A Sinful Heart

Stories of Destructive Love from the Qur'an

YAHYA IBRAHIM

Transcribed and adapted from the lecture
"Open Secrets: Love Stories From The Qur'an"

Published by:

TERTIB PUBLISHING

Unit No. E-10-5, Jalan SS 15/4G, Subang Square,
47500 Subang Jaya, Selangor, Malaysia
+603-5612-2407 (office) / +6017-399-7411 (mobile)
info@tertib.press
www.tertib.press
@tertibpress (Facebook & Instagram)

Author	:	Yahya Ibrahim
Transcriber & Editor	:	Ilyana Elisa
Proofreader	:	Arisha Mohd Affendy
		Hanis Husna Adzhar
Cover designer	:	Abdul Adzim Md Daim
Typesetter	:	Abdul Adzim Md Daim

A SINFUL HEART: STORIES OF DESTRUCTIVE LOVE FROM THE QUR'AN

First Edition: January 2025

Perpustakaan Negara Malaysia
Cataloguing-in-Publication Data
A catalogue record for this book is available from the National Library of Malaysia

ISBN: 978-967-2844-44-0)

Contents

Preface 1

Part 1: Beauty of the Qur'an 4

Chapter 1: Defining the Qur'an 5

Chapter 2: Qur'an as a *Dhikr* 14

Chapter 3: Miraculous *Ayah* 21

Chapter 4: Open Secret 25

Chapter 5: Stories from the Qur'an 31

Part 2: Stories of Destructive Love 34

Chapter 6: Love of Pride 35

Chapter 7: Love of Foreverness 47

Chapter 8: Love Without Effort 58

Chapter 9: Love to Control 66

Chapter 10: Love of Conflict 77

Chapter 11: Love That is Misguided 84

Chapter 12: Love of *Kufr* 97

Chapter 13: Love of Defiance 105

Chapter 14: Love Without Restraint 109

Preface

Bismillāhirraḥmānirraḥīm.

Love, in all its manifestations, is a force that shapes destinies, builds civilisations, and unites hearts. But what happens when love becomes a source of destruction? What happens when it transforms into an obsession, a false idol, or a path away from Allah's guidance? This book, "A Sinful Heart: Stories of Destructive Love from the Qur'an," seeks to explore these questions by delving into the timeless narratives and profound lessons embedded in the Qur'an. It unpacks the beauty, complexity, and moral depth of divine revelation, offering readers a lens through which to reflect on their own hearts and their relationship with Allah (s.w.t.).

The Qur'an is replete with stories that highlight the many shades of human emotion, intention, and action. Among these, love—both its purity and its distortions—stands out as a recurring theme. Whether it is the love of power, the yearning for immortality, or misguided affection, the Qur'an masterfully illustrates how these impulses can either elevate the soul or lead it astray. This book examines such stories to shed light on the nuanced interplay between love and destruction, as well as the consequences of straying from Allah's path.

The first chapters of this book explore the inherent beauty and divine wisdom of the Qur'an, showcasing its literary elegance, profound symbolism, and moral teachings. These chapters set the stage for deeper reflection on the transformative power of love—both when it aligns with divine guidance and when it deviates from it.

The heart of this book lies in its analysis of destructive love, divided into thematic chapters that unpack the complexities of this universal emotion. Each of these chapters examines a form of destructive love that is portrayed through a narrative in the Qur'an and how it leads to the inescapable downfall of the sinful character.

Yet, the Qur'an does not leave us in despair. The final chapters offer hope and guidance, illustrating love's redemptive and righteous forms through the stories of the wife of Fir'awn, Yusuf (a.s.) and more.

Each chapter weaves Qur'anic narratives with contemporary reflections, urging readers to look inward and evaluate their own hearts in light of Allah's guidance. In examining these stories of destructive and redemptive love, this book invites you to embark on a journey of self-discovery and spiritual growth. By confronting the darker impulses within us, we can illuminate the path to a love that is pure, purposeful, and aligned with the pleasure of Allah (s.w.t.).

May Allah (s.w.t.) guide us to cultivate hearts that love rightly, reject what is destructive, and seek His eternal mercy and pleasure above all else. *Āmīn.*

PART 1

Beauty of the Qur'an

CHAPTER 1

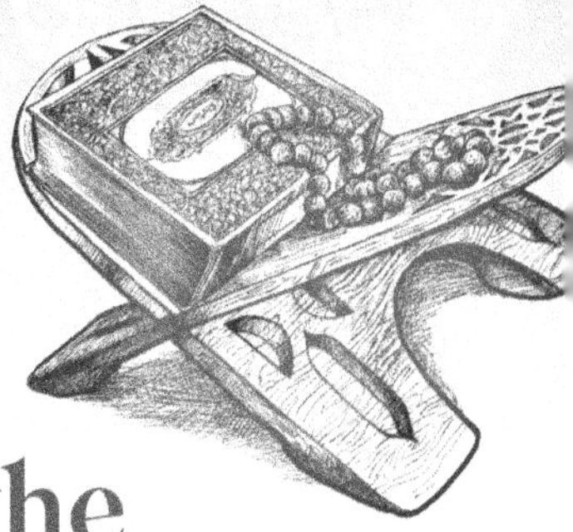

Defining the Qur'an

When discussing about the Qur'an, it is important for us to first begin by defining it and there are four parts of the definition of the Qur'an:

1. ***Kalamullāh***
2. ***Al-munazzal 'ala Muḥammad***
3. ***Al-muta'abbadu bitilawatih***
4. ***Al-mahfuẓ fiṣ-ṣudur wal-maṣaḥif***

1. *Kalamullāh*

The first part of the definition is that it is the spoken words of Allah (s.w.t.)—*kalamullāh*. It is Allah's words, His speech to us. If we were to take the definition only at this level, it is enough.

Allah (s.w.t.) does not reveal Himself for our eyes to behold, because we are not in a realm, not in a place and in a structure that is able to withstand the *Jalal*, the Majesty of Allah (s.w.t.). Allah (s.w.t.) also does not reveal Himself to us audibly, although He has to others before us; Musa *kalimullāh*. However, Allah (s.w.t.) reveals Himself to us in a testament that is meant to be personal and collective at the same time, and this testament is meant to be a completion to all that was revealed beforehand—the Qur'an. It is a seal and a completion, a reiteration that sets aside any previous corruption to the truth that we know today.

If you have ever visited the Sistine Chapel in Rome—the heart of Christians—you will find many icons and statues, and this makes us appreciate our religion, Islam, because we only worship the One true God which is Allah (s.w.t.). *Alḥamdulillāh* for Islam.

In Rome, you can also find a sculpture of Musa (a.s.) by Michelangelo. His impression of Musa (a.s.) is portrayed in his white sculpture of what he, in his mind, believed Musa (a.s.) to look like from what is written in their Christian description. What I found strange was that he sculpted Musa (a.s.) with two horns. This is because in the Bible, in the *Tawrah*, it is said that Musa (a.s.) had the *qaran*. In Semitic languages such as Aramaic and Hebrew, *qaran* means something that protrudes. What is meant by it is that light shines from the face of Musa (a.s.), but when they translated it from the original language, the translator made a mistake. He translated *qaran*—originally meaning light or *nur*—to horns like a sheep. So when Michelangelo wanted to make a sculpture of Musa (a.s.), he made a picture in his mind of a man with horns.

Look at how Allah (s.w.t.) subtly exposes the beauty of the Qur'an. It is incredible how Allah (s.w.t.) has preserved the Qur'an for us. Allah (s.w.t.) says, "I brought down this reminder to you, Muḥammad. I will be the One who protects it."

إِنَّا نَحْنُ نَزَّلْنَا ٱلذِّكْرَ وَإِنَّا لَهُۥ لَحَٰفِظُونَ ﴿٩﴾

Indeed, it is We who sent down the message [i.e., the Qur'an], and indeed, We will be its guardian.

(Surah al-Ḥijr, 15:9)

The Malay version of the Qur'an is not Qur'an. It is someone's understanding of the Qur'an. The

Qur'an is the word of Allah (s.w.t.) that has been preserved in the way it was initially revealed to Prophet Muḥammad (s.a.w.). This is *kalamullāh.*

If we were to ask a Christian pastor, "Is the Bible God's word?" The answer would be, "Yes." Then we ask, "Did God literally say these phrases?" They will say, "No. This is the meaning, the understanding, and the usage of God's word. This is God's intent for us."

Then, we have our Qur'an. *Kāf Hā Yā 'Ayn Sād* and *Alif Lām Mīm*. These are letters in the first verse of some surahs. Could you imagine a Christian pastor standing in church and reciting, "X G Q R S." We would think that he is out of his mind. On the other hand, you have no problem with me reciting *Kāf Hā Yā 'Ayn Sād* for surah Maryam and *Alif Lām Mīm* for surah al-Baqarah, because we believe differently from what they believe. We believe that every letter is from Allah (s.w.t.). There is no English translation for these letters. Can a Muslim begin *ṣalah* and instead of reciting *Ṭā Hā* for example, they begin with the second verse? No. Others will say, "Hey, you missed the first *ayah*." It is the Qur'an. It is *kalamullāh*. It is unchangeable and incorruptible. There is no tolerance for it.

2. *Al-munazzal ʿala Muḥammad*

The Qur'an is revealed and brought down to our Prophet Muḥammad (s.a.w.). It is not from this world and this is why we honour the words of Allah (s.w.t.). This is also why many of the surahs begin with *tanzil*. For example:

تَنزِيلُ ٱلْكِتَـٰبِ مِنَ ٱللَّهِ ٱلْعَزِيزِ ٱلْحَكِيمِ ﴿٢﴾

The revelation of the Book is from Allah, the Exalted in Might, the Wise.

(Surah al-Aḥqaf, 46:2)

The Qur'an is a revelation that is brought down from the Lord of all realms and all existence. Attached to it is the name and the persona of the individual Prophet Muḥammad (s.a.w.). There is no Qur'an without Prophet Muḥammad (s.a.w.). There is no *lā ʾilāha ʾilla-llāh*, except *muḥammadur-rasūlu-llāh*. Someone will correct us. We cannot just say, "*Ashhadu allā ʾilāha ʾilla-llāh*," and then stop. Others will look at us and say, "You're halfway, *wa ʾashhadu ʾanna muḥammadur-rasūlu-llāh*."

3. *Al-muta'abbadu bitilawatih*

We earn reward with each reading, each recitation and by looking into the script of the Qur'an:

> Narrated Muḥammad bin Ka'b Al-Quraẓi:
>
> I heard 'Abdullah bin Mas'ud saying: "The Messenger of Allah (s.a.w.) said: '[Whoever recites a letter] from Allah's Book, then he receives the reward from it, and the reward of ten the like of it. I do not say that *Alif Lām Mīm* is a letter, but *Alif* is a letter, *Lām* is a letter and *Mīm* is a letter.'"
>
> (Jami' at-Tirmidhi 2910)

There is no other text in the world that we read three letters and it earns us thirty *ḥasanat*. *Alif*, *Lām* and *Mīm* are one letter each and we earn one *ḥasanah* for each letter. Then, every *ḥasanah* is rewarded ten times. So, we earn thirty *ḥasanat* when we recite *Alif Lām Mīm*—which is an act of worship. It is also an act of worship to look at the script of the Qur'an and to write it.

4. *Al-maḥfuẓ fiṣ-ṣudur wal-maṣaḥif*

The Qur'an is guarded and protected in the heart of the Muslim community and in the *muṣḥaf*:

وَلَقَدْ يَسَّرْنَا ٱلْقُرْءَانَ لِلذِّكْرِ فَهَلْ مِن مُّدَّكِرٍ ﴿٣٢﴾

> And We have certainly made the Qur'an easy for remembrance, so is there any who will remember?
>
> (Surah al-Qamar, 54:32)

The integral component of Allah's protection of the Qur'an is us, ourselves. If I were to recite the Qur'an and make a mistake in my recitation, someone would stop me, even in *ṣalah*. They would say, "Hey! Don't mess around with the word of Allah (s.w.t.)," even if it is a letter, even if it is a vowel, and even if it is an error in *shaddah*.

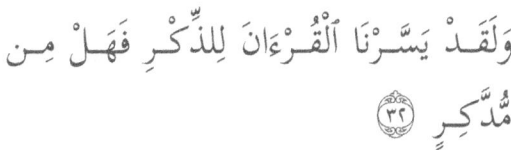

If someone was to lead you in *ṣalah* and they make a mistake in surah al-Fatiḥah intentionally, would you re-do the *ṣalah*? They read, for example, "*'Iyāka na'budu waiyyāka nasta'īn*," instead of, "*'Iyyāka na'budu waiyyāka*

nasta'īn." There is a difference in the recitation of *'Iyyāka* and this difference creates a huge impact in the meaning of the *ayah. 'Iyāka na'bud* means, "The sun sets, I turn to in worship." The correct recitation is *'iyyāka na'bud*, "Only You Allah I worship."

When our *ustadh* stresses us in *tajwid*, it is because of *maḥfuẓ*—the Qur'an is protected by Allah (s.w.t.) through it. Imagine the honour bestowed upon a person who teaches the Qur'an. The Prophet (s.a.w.) said:

Narrated 'Uthman:

> The Prophet (s.a.w.) said, "The best among you (Muslims) are those who learn the Qur'an and teach it."
>
> (Ṣaḥiḥ al-Bukhari 5027)

The best of us is the one who learns the Qur'an by dedicating energy, time, minutes, hours, weeks, months and years to the book of Allah (s.w.t.) but does not stop and keep it, instead they share it with others. The Prophet (s.a.w.) said:

'Abdullah bin 'Amr bin Al-'Aṣ (r.a.) reported:

> The Prophet (s.a.w.) said, "Convey from me even an *ayah* of the Qur'an..."
>
> (Riyaḍ aṣ-Ṣaliḥin 1380)

The Prophet (s.a.w.) did not tell us to transmit from him a hadith, but an *ayah* of the Qur'an. It is not, "Transmit from me, my words," but, "Transmit from me, even one *ayah* from the book of Allah." The sunnah and the traditions are only reinforcing the Qur'an brought down by Allah (s.w.t.).

CHAPTER 2

Qur'an as a *Dhikr*

As we unravel the secrets of the Qur'an, we come to understand that its language is beautiful. Its scope is wide. Its essence is that it is meant to be a *dhikr*:

وَإِنَّهُۥ لَذِكْرٌ لَّكَ وَلِقَوْمِكَ ۖ وَسَوْفَ تُسْـَٔلُونَ ﴿٤٤﴾

And indeed, it is a remembrance for you and your people, and you [all] are going to be questioned.

(Surah az-Zukhruf, 43:44)

When Allah (s.w.t.) uses the word *dhikr*, it is a remembrance—a reminder. We are described by

Allah (s.w.t.) as being *insan*:

خَلَقَ ٱلْإِنسَٰنَ ﴿٣﴾

Created man.

(Surah ar-Raḥman, 55:3)

Humanity, we are *insan*. We are prone to *nisyan*; forgetfulness. The word *insan* comes from *nasa*, which means to forget. Allah (s.w.t.) says about Adam (a.s.), "I gave Adam instructions, but he forgot."

وَلَقَدْ عَهِدْنَآ إِلَىٰٓ ءَادَمَ مِن قَبْلُ فَنَسِىَ
وَلَمْ نَجِدْ لَهُۥ عَزْمًا ﴿١١٥﴾

And We had already taken a promise from Adam before, but he forgot; and We found not in him determination.

(Surah Ṭaha, 20:115)

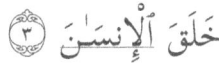

One of the deficiencies that we have is that we are forgetful of our relationship with Allah (s.w.t.), so He sent reminders through His people, His scriptures and His orders, and His final reminder is through the Qur'an—the book of Allah (s.w.t.). It affirms the trueness of what came before us and it informs us about what will come after us—the Day of Judgement.

Whenever Allah (s.w.t.) uses the word *dhikr* in the Qur'an, there are particular meanings that are attached to it. First, it means Allah (s.w.t.) is telling us something new, something we do not know yet. So every time we open the Qur'an, there is going to be something new that we may learn:

وَٱذْكُرْ فِى ٱلْكِتَٰبِ مُوسَىٰٓ ۚ إِنَّهُۥ كَانَ مُخْلَصًا وَكَانَ رَسُولًا نَّبِيًّا ﴿٥١﴾

And mention in the Book, Musa. Indeed, he was chosen, and he was a messenger and a prophet.

(Surah Maryam, 19:51)

Second, Allah (s.w.t.) reminds us of something we knew but forgot, such as Allah (s.w.t.) says to us, "Don't forget. Here's the reminder in the Book about such and such."

وَلَقَدْ أَرْسَلْنَا مُوسَىٰ بِـَٔايَـٰتِنَآ أَنْ أَخْرِجْ قَوْمَكَ مِنَ ٱلظُّلُمَـٰتِ إِلَى ٱلنُّورِ وَذَكِّرْهُم بِأَيَّىٰمِ ٱللَّهِ ۚ إِنَّ فِى ذَٰلِكَ لَـَٔايَـٰتٍ لِّكُلِّ صَبَّارٍ شَكُورٍ ۝٥

And We certainly sent Musa with Our signs, [saying], "Bring out your people from darknesses into the light and remind them of the days of Allah." Indeed in that are signs for everyone patient and grateful.

(Surah Ibrahim, 14:5)

Next, Allah (s.w.t.) uses the Qur'an to remind us of something we ignore. It is like a wake-up call, "You know this but you're trying to pretend you don't. Remember it. Don't pretend that you have forgotten and don't ignore it."

وَٱذْكُر رَّبَّكَ فِى نَفْسِكَ تَضَرُّعًا وَخِيفَةً
وَدُونَ ٱلْجَهْرِ مِنَ ٱلْقَوْلِ بِٱلْغُدُوِّ وَٱلْءَاصَالِ
وَلَا تَكُن مِّنَ ٱلْغَٰفِلِينَ ٢٠٥

And remember your Lord within yourself in humility and in fear without being apparent in speech—in the mornings and the evenings. And do not be among the heedless.

(Surah al-Aʿraf, 7:205)

Other than that, Allah (s.w.t.) wants us to face what is inconvenient for us that we are trying to avoid. There are certain things in the Qur'an that are inconvenient truths. These truths are going to change something in us if we face them. We are going to have to make changes to our lives, changes in our attitudes and behaviours. So, Allah (s.w.t.) is saying there are certain things that may inconvenience us, but we should face them instead of avoiding them:

وَلَا تَنكِحُوا۟ ٱلْمُشْرِكَٰتِ حَتَّىٰ يُؤْمِنَّ ۚ وَلَأَمَةٌ
مُّؤْمِنَةٌ خَيْرٌ مِّن مُّشْرِكَةٍ وَلَوْ أَعْجَبَتْكُمْ ۗ وَلَا

تُنكِحُوا۟ ٱلْمُشْرِكِينَ حَتَّىٰ يُؤْمِنُوا۟ ۚ وَلَعَبْدٌ
مُّؤْمِنٌ خَيْرٌ مِّن مُّشْرِكٍ وَلَوْ أَعْجَبَكُمْ ۗ
أُو۟لَـٰٓئِكَ يَدْعُونَ إِلَى ٱلنَّارِ ۖ وَٱللَّهُ يَدْعُوٓا۟ إِلَى
ٱلْجَنَّةِ وَٱلْمَغْفِرَةِ بِإِذْنِهِۦ ۖ وَيُبَيِّنُ ءَايَـٰتِهِۦ لِلنَّاسِ
لَعَلَّهُمْ يَتَذَكَّرُونَ ﴿٢٢١﴾

And do not marry polytheistic women until they believe. And a believing slave woman is better than a polytheist, even though she might please you. And do not marry polytheistic men [to your women] until they believe. And a believing slave is better than a polytheist, even though he might please you. Those invite [you] to the Fire, but Allah invites to Paradise and to forgiveness, by His permission. And He makes clear His verses [i.e., ordinances] to the people that perhaps they may remember.

(Surah al-Baqarah, 2:221)

Finally, it is meant to inspire us. The Qur'an, as a *dhikr*, is meant to be a divine inspiration—*waḥyu*. It is Allah's communication and inspiration to us as human beings through our Prophet Muḥammad (s.a.w.):

إِنْ هُوَ إِلَّا ذِكْرٌ لِّلْعَٰلَمِينَ ﴿٨٧﴾

It is but a reminder to the worlds.

(Surah Ṣad, 38:87)

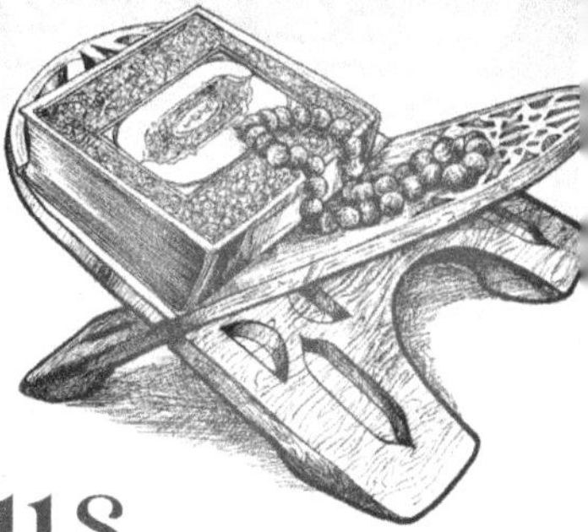

CHAPTER 3

Miraculous *Ayah*

Every *ayah* is a miraculous statement in the Qur'an. Certain verses of the Qur'an may be a miracle for me, but not for you. This is why every *ayah* may have different reactions with different people.

I grew up in a Western non-Muslim public school in Canada. I was maybe sixteen years old and had just begun my journey with the Qur'an. I had a *muṣḥaf* that was one of the old Madinah copies, and it had an English translation. My Qur'an teacher—may Allah (s.w.t.) have mercy upon him—said to me, "Yahya, you should familiarise yourself with the Qur'an, not just how to read it, but also to understand some of its meaning. We'll learn more of it as you go on, but what I want you to do is to read the English translation two or three times while you are memorising the verses."

And I had a friend who would visit my home on odd occasions. He was always very polite and a little bit different to some of my other friends who were non-Muslims. We came back from school one day and my Qur'an was on my desk in my room. I went out of my room to ask my mother to make food for us. As I was gone, my friend was standing at my desk and reading the Qur'an. When I came back into the room, he was in tears. He asked, "What is this?" I looked and said, "Oh, that's the Qur'an. What's wrong?" He replied, "I got scared." So I asked him, "What happened?"

I had never seen that kind of reaction before. He said, "This is the truth. This is correct." The surah that I was memorising during that time was surah an-Nisa'. The verses did not affect me, but he read it for thirty seconds—literally, thirty seconds—and became a Muslim. He said, "I want to be this." I replied, "It's called Islam." Then he said, "This is the truth." So I asked, "What part of it?" And he had his finger on the *ayah*:

إِنَّ ٱلَّذِينَ يَأْكُلُونَ أَمْوَٰلَ ٱلْيَتَٰمَىٰ ظُلْمًا
إِنَّمَا يَأْكُلُونَ فِى بُطُونِهِمْ نَارًا ۖ ... ﴿١٠﴾

Indeed, those who devour the property of orphans unjustly are only consuming into their bellies fire…

(Surah an-Nisa', 4:10)

What I did not know was that he was an orphan and had been in foster care. Every family that looked after him had treated him unjustly. The money that the government gave for them to buy him clothes or books and other necessities was taken by them. They never gave him an allowance, they never bought for him what he deserved. He always had to scrounge around and find a way to survive. When he would ask for what was his right, he would be abused for it and he would be yelled at. So the moment his eyes saw that *ayah*, it changed the rest of his life—he became a Muslim because of it.

One *ayah.* We might not feel anything when reading it, but that one *ayah* could potentially change someone else's life, and that is the beauty of the

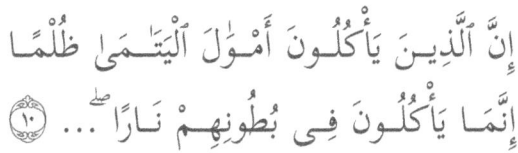

Qur'an. What verse is relevant to us that we have not become familiar with yet? What story of the Qur'an could resonate with us if we engage with the word of Allah (s.w.t.)? We would miss out on transforming our whole lives because of our detachment with the Qur'an. And what *ayah* contains our *hidayah* that will unlock incredible potential, success, opportunity and change if we would just turn the key?

CHAPTER 4

Open Secret

One of my teachers shared this blessed teaching and I want you, dear readers, to think about it: there is no surah in the Qur'an—there is no chapter in the Qur'an—except in it is a word or verse that is not found in any other surah. Even the shortest surah has this feature:

إِنَّآ أَعْطَيْنَٰكَ ٱلْكَوْثَرَ ﴿١﴾ فَصَلِّ لِرَبِّكَ
وَٱنْحَرْ ﴿٢﴾ إِنَّ شَانِئَكَ هُوَ ٱلْأَبْتَرُ ﴿٣﴾

Indeed, We have granted you, [O' Muḥammad], *al-Kawthar*. So pray to your Lord and offer sacrifice [to Him alone]. Indeed, your enemy is the one cut off.

(Surah al-Kawthar, 108:1-3)

Nowhere else in the Qur'an the word *shāni'aka* is used.

Nowhere else in the Qur'an the word *al-abtar* is used.

Nowhere else in the Qur'an the word *al-Kawthar* is used.

Every ayah in this shortest surah of the Qur'an has a sign to us of Allah's use of language in a way that human beings cannot construct. He makes usage of a term, a verb or a noun that is found nowhere else in the Qur'an. Every surah in the Qur'an has in it unique verses, unique words and unique descriptions that are never repeated again. Allah (s.w.t.) says:

وَلَوْ أَنَّمَا فِى ٱلْأَرْضِ مِن شَجَرَةٍ أَقْلَٰمٌ
وَٱلْبَحْرُ يَمُدُّهُۥ مِنۢ بَعْدِهِۦ سَبْعَةُ أَبْحُرٍ
مَّا نَفِدَتْ كَلِمَٰتُ ٱللَّهِ ۗ إِنَّ ٱللَّهَ عَزِيزٌ
حَكِيمٌ ﴿٢٧﴾

And if whatever trees upon the earth were pens and the sea [was ink], replenished thereafter by seven [more] seas, the words of Allah would not be exhausted. Indeed, Allah is Exalted in Might and Wise.

(Surah Luqman, 31:27)

Even if all of the trees were turned to pens and all of the oceans were turned to ink, His words to us would never, ever, come to an end. The oceans would dry up, the trees would be cut down, and all of the pens and ink would be used up, but He would still be able to communicate a message to us that has not already been spoken. There is a beauty in understanding that our *ummah* is the final one receiving this message.

One of the things that some of my non-native Arabic students struggle with is understanding the Qur'an. They would say, "Shaykh Yahya, you're an Arab. Maybe for you the Qur'an is easy. It should be second nature." I say, "You don't understand." Do you think the average Arab person can pick up the Qur'an and read it like a newspaper? No. Only certain words, yes.

Why do we have Tafsir Ibn Kathir, Tafsir al-Baghawi, Tafsir al-Razi and many more *tafsirs*? *Tafsir* means an interpretation of the Qur'an to help us understand its meaning. It is easy for us to read the Qur'an. Everyone can read its translation in any language, but the context is ambiguous. Not everyone can understand the context. The Qur'an requires study.

Even the *ṣaḥabah* needed someone to interpret the verses of the Qur'an. Allah (s.w.t.) revealed:

...ٱلْيَوْمَ أَكْمَلْتُ لَكُمْ دِينَكُمْ وَأَتْمَمْتُ عَلَيْكُمْ نِعْمَتِى وَرَضِيتُ لَكُمُ ٱلْإِسْلَٰمَ دِينًا ۚ...﴿٣﴾

> ...This day I have perfected for you your religion and completed My favour upon you and have approved for you Islam as religion....
>
> (Surah al-Ma'idah, 5:3)

Abu Bakr (r.a.) started weeping. The *ṣaḥabah* saw him weeping and asked, "What's wrong with the old man who's crying today? What happened? We don't understand."

Narrated Abu Sa'id al-Khudri:

> Allah's Messenger (s.a.w.) addressed the people saying, "Allah has given option to a slave to choose this world or what is with Him. The slave has chosen what is with Allah." Abu Bakr wept, and we were astonished at his weeping caused by what the Prophet (s.a.w.) mentioned as to a Slave (of Allah) who had been offered a choice, (we learned later on) that Allah's Messenger (s.a.w.) himself was

> the person who was given the choice, and that Abu Bakr knew best of all of us. Allah's Messenger (s.a.w.) added, "The person who has favoured me most of all both with his company and wealth, is Abu Bakr. If I were to take a *khalil* other than my Lord, I would have taken Abu Bakr as such, but (what relates us) is the Islamic brotherhood and friendliness. All the gates of the Mosque should be closed except the gate of Abu Bakr."
>
> (Ṣaḥiḥ al-Bukhari 3654)

It was on the Day of 'Arafah during the final *ḥajj* of the Prophet (s.a.w.) that Abu Bakr (r.a.) was weeping, because the completion of Islam means there is no more need for the Messenger (s.a.w.).

The Qur'an is an open secret. It is open because we can read it at any time, but it is also a secret because we need to study it further for us to understand it. We need to give it our attention, we need to give it our focus.

CHAPTER 5

Stories from the Qur'an

One of the interesting areas of the Qur'an that we always come back to is the stories of the Qur'an. The stories are always passed on as if they are bedtime stories, but this is not how we should do it. Each narrative in the Qur'an, whether about the lives of the prophets or others—whether righteous or immoral—is meant for us to reflect on ourselves and encourage us to change our behaviour to what is pleasing to Allah (s.w.t.).

The stories in the Qur'an are not meant to be idolised. They are meant for us to reflect on our behaviour, change of our behaviour, change of our circumstances; as an individual, as a community and as a society. This is what we aim for through our discussion of some of the familial and love relationships in the Qur'an.

In this book, I would like to discuss mainly about the destructive love stories from the Qur'an; the love stories that brought ruin.

Love is powerful, love is important.

Allah (s.w.t.) gives special consideration in particular to relationships in the Qur'an. Every Prophet and every Messenger, they all have these very complex relationships that are meant to mimic anything that we in society could ever encounter:

Competitive jealousy that caused brothers to seek to end the life of one of their own; the brothers of Yusuf (a.s.).

A long-distance father who could only see his son every so often; Ibrahim (a.s.) and Isma'il (a.s.).

A relationship of brothers who cooperated upon the truth; Musa (a.s.) and Harun (a.s.).

An abused wife in a home of tyranny; Asiyah (r.a.), the wife of Fir'awn.

A betraying spouse to an honourable man; the wife of Nuḥ (a.s.) and the wife of Luṭ (a.s.).

All of these and many other stories are meant to inspire reflection on our relationship with Allah (s.w.t.). There are also characters in the Qur'an who were not prophets and Messengers, but we can still take their stories for further study to reflect on the relationship that we have with Allah (s.w.t.).

PART 2

Stories of Destructive Love

CHAPTER 6

Love of Pride

The Pride of *Iblis*

The very first story told in the Qur'an is the story of *Iblis*. This is not a coincidence. Allah (s.w.t.) gives us the example of a creation before our creation.

I want you to understand as human beings, as Muslims, we do not have an agitated position against science and nature—against the study of anthropology, human expanse and evolution on earth. There were other creations who lived on earth before human beings. There was the creation of the unseen world.

The word *jinn* comes from ج (*jim*) and ن (*nun*). They are the same letters that spell *Jannah*. What does *Jannah* mean?

فَلَمَّا جَنَّ عَلَيْهِ ٱلَّيْلُ رَءَا كَوْكَبًا ۖ... ﴿٧٦﴾

So when the night covered him [with darkness], he saw a star…

(Surah al-Anʿam, 6:76)

In the verse above, *janna* is translated as "covered"; Ibrahim (a.s.) was sitting when the night covered him. The word *jinn* is a descriptive word. It is anything that is unseen to us that we know exists.

The word *Jannah* means that when we see it from the outside, it is so lush and full of foliage. We do not know what is in it. No eye has seen it, no ear has heard its delight and no human being could imagine it—*Jannah*. It is purely translated as "garden." It has indescribable beauty:

Narrated Abu Hurayrah:

The Prophet (s.a.w.) said, "Allah said, 'I have prepared for My righteous slaves (such excellent things) as no eye has ever seen, nor an ear has ever heard nor a human heart can ever think of.'"

(Ṣaḥiḥ al-Bukhari 7498)

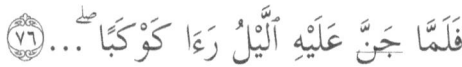

Jinn, or more specifically *Iblis*, is from those who are unseen to us in this life. They can see and view us, and have access to us from where we cannot see them:

...إِنَّهُۥ يَرَىٰكُمْ هُوَ وَقَبِيلُهُۥ مِنْ حَيْثُ لَا تَرَوْنَهُمْ ۗ... ﴿٢٧﴾

...Indeed, he sees you, he and his tribe, from where you do not see them...

(Surah al-Aʿraf, 7:27)

They are an intelligent creation of Allah (s.w.t.) that have different laws to their nature. They were not created from the essence of the elements of this earth. We—human beings—were created from the element of this earth, whereas the *jinn* were created from a source of energy—fire. They are different to us, but known to Allah (s.w.t.). *Wallāhu aʿlam.*

وَلَقَدْ خَلَقْنَا ٱلْإِنسَٰنَ مِن صَلْصَٰلٍ مِّنْ حَمَإٍ مَّسْنُونٍ ﴿٢٦﴾ وَٱلْجَآنَّ خَلَقْنَٰهُ مِن قَبْلُ مِن نَّارِ ٱلسَّمُومِ ﴿٢٧﴾

> And We did certainly create man out of clay from an altered black mud. And the *jinn* We created before from scorching fire.
>
> (Surah al-Ḥijr, 15:26-27)

There were other creations before Adam (a.s.), who walked, talked, ate and lived in communities in their own limited capacities. What makes us different is that Allah (s.w.t.) describes us as having a cognitive quality. We are *insan*; we may forget our relationship with Allah (s.w.t.), but we are thinking.

Allah (s.w.t.) also describes us as *bashar*:

وَلَقَدْ نَعْلَمُ أَنَّهُمْ يَقُولُونَ إِنَّمَا يُعَلِّمُهُۥ بَشَرٌ ۗ... ﴿١٠٣﴾

> And We certainly know that they say, "It is only a human being who teaches him [i.e., the Prophet (s.a.w.)]"...
>
> (Surah an-Naḥl, 16:103)

The physical description Allah (s.w.t.) gives us as human beings is *bashar*; our skin shows. One of the things that separates us from other creations that walk the earth is we are furless. When we look at some of the fossils people have discovered, they claim Lucy—a hairy ape—is what the early humans looked like, but this is wrong. Adam (a.s.) is the first of Adam, the first of us. Adam (a.s.) is different.

Allah (s.w.t.) said to the angels, "I'm going to put on the earth one who will now inherit it."

وَإِذْ قَالَ رَبُّكَ لِلْمَلَـٰٓئِكَةِ إِنِّى جَاعِلٌ فِى ٱلْأَرْضِ خَلِيفَةً ۖ... ﴿٣٠﴾

And [mention, O' Muḥammad], when your Lord said to the angels, "Indeed, I will make upon the earth a successive authority..."

(Surah al-Baqarah, 2:30)

Inherit it from who? From the others who were already there. Humanity will overcome them, humanity will take charge, humanity will subdue everything else:

...هُوَ أَنشَأَكُم مِّنَ ٱلْأَرْضِ وَٱسْتَعْمَرَكُمْ
فِيهَا فَٱسْتَغْفِرُوهُ ثُمَّ تُوبُوٓا۟ إِلَيْهِ ۚ إِنَّ رَبِّى
قَرِيبٌ مُّجِيبٌ ﴿٦١﴾

"...He has produced you from the earth and settled you in it, so ask forgiveness of Him and then repent to Him. Indeed, my Lord is near and responsive."

(Surah Hud, 11:61)

We are different from what was already there. When the angels were told, "I will place on the earth *khalifah*," they responded, "O' Allah, will you put on the earth that which will cause corruption like we're already seeing? There are already these ones who are brutal and they shed blood. Are you going to put upon the earth as we see already?"

...قَالُوٓا۟ أَتَجْعَلُ فِيهَا مَن يُفْسِدُ فِيهَا
وَيَسْفِكُ ٱلدِّمَآءَ وَنَحْنُ نُسَبِّحُ بِحَمْدِكَ
وَنُقَدِّسُ لَكَ ۖ... ﴿٣٠﴾

> …They said, "Will You place upon it one who causes corruption therein and sheds blood, while we exalt You with praise and declare Your perfection?"…
>
> (Surah al-Baqarah, 2:30)

Allah (s.w.t.) said, "I know of what will come of them that you do not know." In other words, Allah (s.w.t.) was saying, "Your observable knowledge of what has already happened is different to My eternal knowledge of what will be the eventuality of mankind, different to others."

…قَالَ إِنِّيٓ أَعۡلَمُ مَا لَا تَعۡلَمُونَ ٣٠

> …He [Allah] said, "Indeed, I know that which you do not know."
>
> (Surah al-Baqarah, 2:30)

After the creation of Adam (a.s.), Allah (s.w.t.) introduces the story of *Iblis*. Allah (s.w.t.) ordered, "Fall down in submission, *sujud* to Adam."

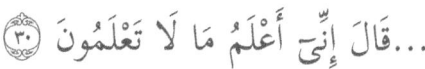

فَإِذَا سَوَّيْتُهُۥ وَنَفَخْتُ فِيهِ مِن رُّوحِى فَقَعُوا۟ لَهُۥ سَٰجِدِينَ ﴿٧٢﴾

"So when I have proportioned him and breathed into him of My [created] soul, then fall down to him in prostration."

(Surah Ṣad, 38:72)

The best and noblest of creatures, and everything under them were now subdued to the authority of Adam (a.s.)—except *Iblis*. He departed with arrogance and pride, with love for himself that blinded him to the order of Allah (s.w.t.):

فَسَجَدَ ٱلْمَلَٰٓئِكَةُ كُلُّهُمْ أَجْمَعُونَ ﴿٧٣﴾ إِلَّآ إِبْلِيسَ ٱسْتَكْبَرَ وَكَانَ مِنَ ٱلْكَٰفِرِينَ ﴿٧٤﴾

So the angels prostrated—all of them entirely. Except *Iblis*; he was arrogant and became among the disbelievers.

(Surah Ṣad, 38:73-74)

The Lesson

قَالَ أَنَا خَيْرٌ مِّنْهُ ۖ خَلَقْتَنِي مِن نَّارٍ وَخَلَقْتَهُۥ مِن طِينٍ ﴿٧٦﴾

He said, "I am better than him. You created me from fire and created him from clay."

(Surah Ṣad, 38:76)

When we love ourselves too much, when we regard ourselves too high like *Iblis*, and when we hold ourselves higher than others in any capacity—in our faithfulness to God, in our academic pursuit, in our financial matters, whatever it is—we cannot envision that someone is able to exceed us, to the point we cannot be accepting, wanting, maybe even praying for someone to achieve success because we could not achieve it.

This is the basis of envy, which is the poison of *Iblis*. *Iblis*' most worrisome trait is that he has *ḥasad*. He looked at Adam (a.s.) and said, "Why him and not me? Why wasn't this order for me when I was brought in?" *Iblis* knew Allah (s.w.t.) and he worshipped Allah (s.w.t.). He said, "My Lord, I know You, Allah. Why not me? I view myself more favourably than others. I find in me that I am better than him."

Do you know what the irony of *Kursi* is? The creation of fire is more noble than that of dust. On a logical level, *Iblis* is correct, but this is not what is important.

For example, in my home, we have a fireplace but not a mudplace. We do not walk into the house with mud on our shoes, but we might light a candle to create a romantic atmosphere. Even if it is hot, we have the background of the fireplace on the TV. It is not even a real fire, but we want the look of the regal dancing of the flame. It is noble. Fire gives heat and warmth, and it helps us with cooking.

Iblis is not illogical in his assessment, "I'm from something more noble than this. You have preferred this to me?"

قَالَ أَرَءَيْتَكَ هَٰذَا ٱلَّذِى كَرَّمْتَ عَلَىَّ... ﴿٦٢﴾

[*Iblis*] said, "Do You see this one whom You have honoured above me?"...

(Surah al-Isra', 17:62)

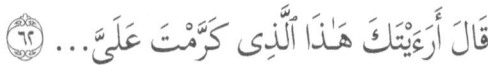

What causes self-love to be so destructive is it makes one forget that it is not about what is right or what is wrong, what is better or what is worse. It makes one forget that it is the command of Allah (s.w.t.). What causes *Iblis* to fall out of favour with Allah (s.w.t.) is that Allah (s.w.t.) did not say, "Make *sujud* if you are lesser than Adam." Why did Allah (s.w.t.) command the angels, which are better than *Iblis*, to make *sujud* first? Because it is not about the quality that we assess ourselves. It is about the order of Allah (s.w.t.) that is given.

In the study of *tazkiyah*, this ailment of the heart is called *'ujub*; to be self-loving to a fatal point in life that it blinds us to the obligations due between ourselves and Allah (s.w.t.), and between ourselves and others and the orders of Allah (s.w.t.). This destructive love causes a person to hold themselves to a high regard that it blinds them to fulfilling the rights of those who are lesser to them. This becomes a regular theme that we will revisit in the Qur'an.

This is where our focus should be in life. In our marriage, in our friendship with others or in the workplace, sometimes we have this mentality of, "What would they do without me? The whole place will shut down!"

If Bill Gates dies, is Microsoft going to shut down?

Steve Jobs is no longer working at Apple, is Apple still working or actually getting better?

In our families, sometimes we have this mentality of, "What would you do? If I were to divorce you, where would you go? You would live on the streets." But we forget that we are not *ar-Razzāq*.

This destructive self-love ruins homes, ruins happy marriages and ruins future generations of children who grow up seeing someone who they do not respect, because they are not respectable. They do not respect their place between them and Allah (s.w.t.).

May Allah (s.w.t.) have mercy on the believers. May Allah (s.w.t.) have mercy on those who deserve it, *Allāhumma Āmīn.*

This concludes our first story of destructive love, the story of *Iblis*. May Allah (s.w.t.) protect us from this mindset, *Allāhumma Āmīn.*

CHAPTER 7

Love of Foreverness

Adam (a.s.) and the Forbidden Tree

The second story of destructive love is the story of Adam (a.s.). It is a bit surprising that we would use the name of Adam (a.s.) as one that can be used as a story of misplaced love, but the pursuit of foreverness is a human flaw in capacity.

It is the concept of wanting to be in love forever, healthy forever and happy forever—we do not want anything to come in our way, we do not want to experience loss and we want to always be averting any disaster.

Adam's love of foreverness is the story of the tree. Adam (a.s.) was in *Jannah* and Allah (s.w.t.) said,

"You and your spouse, Ḥawwa', enter *Jannah.* Eat and enjoy. Be blessed in all of it whatever you want, but on one condition: do not go near this tree."

وَقُلْنَا يَٰٓـَٔادَمُ ٱسْكُنْ أَنتَ وَزَوْجُكَ ٱلْجَنَّةَ وَكُلَا مِنْهَا رَغَدًا حَيْثُ شِئْتُمَا وَلَا تَقْرَبَا هَٰذِهِ ٱلشَّجَرَةَ فَتَكُونَا مِنَ ٱلظَّٰلِمِينَ ﴿٣٥﴾

And We said, "O' Adam, dwell, you and your wife, in Paradise and eat therefrom in [ease and] abundance from wherever you will. But do not approach this tree, lest you be among the wrongdoers."

(Surah al-Baqarah, 2:35)

It is not "do not eat," not "do not enjoy," but "do not go NEAR it." Whenever Allah (s.w.t.) says do not go near, it is one of the clauses in our *shari'ah* that something is haram. For example:

وَلَا تَقْرَبُوا ٱلزِّنَىٰٓ ۖ إِنَّهُۥ كَانَ فَٰحِشَةً وَسَآءَ سَبِيلًا ﴿٣٢﴾

> And do not approach unlawful sexual intercourse. Indeed, it is ever an immorality and is evil as a way.
>
> (Surah al-Isra', 17:32)

Allah (s.w.t.) does not say do not commit *zina*; Allah (s.w.t.) says do not even go near it. This means we should avoid everything that could lead us towards it whether it is through our gaze, our ears, our speech, or our actions.

So why did Adam (a.s.) go near the tree? The love of foreverness. How did *Iblis* make the tree seem beautiful to Adam (a.s.)? *Iblis* said, "There has to be something special. There has to be a reason."

Are the fruits different? No. Adam (a.s.) kept circling around the tree and when he got closer, *Iblis* said, "Ah, the *khuld* tree. You have all these blessings, Adam. You have all this *ni'mah*, but it can be taken away from you. Look at what happened to me."

The test of *Iblis* is also for Adam (a.s.). When *Iblis* was dethroned, it was a signal to Adam (a.s.). Allah (s.w.t.) was signalling, "Pay attention, My *raḥmah* is My *raḥmah*, but My *'adl* is My *'adl*." Justice is justice. Rules are rules.

Why did Allah (s.w.t.) expel *Iblis* in front of Adam (a.s.)?

قَالَ ٱخْرُجْ مِنْهَا مَذْءُومًا مَّدْحُورًا ۖ لَّمَن تَبِعَكَ مِنْهُمْ لَأَمْلَأَنَّ جَهَنَّمَ مِنكُمْ أَجْمَعِينَ ﴿١٨﴾

[Allah] said, "Depart from it [i.e., Paradise], reproached and expelled. Whoever follows you among them—I will surely fill Hell with you, all together."

(Surah al-Aʿraf, 7:18)

It is not so that Adam (a.s.) says, "See? I'm better." It is not for him to be self-deluded that it can never happen to him. It is for him—and also for us—to know that misfortune can happen.

Iblis whispered, "Maybe what is special about this tree is that if you eat from it, it will give you immortality. This *Jannah* that you're in, it will protect you from being like me."

...وَقَالَ مَا نَهَىٰكُمَا رَبُّكُمَا عَنْ هَٰذِهِ ٱلشَّجَرَةِ إِلَّآ أَن تَكُونَا مَلَكَيْنِ أَوْ تَكُونَا مِنَ ٱلْخَٰلِدِينَ ﴿٢٠﴾

...He said, "Your Lord did not forbid you this tree except that you become angels or become of the immortal."

(Surah al-Aʿraf, 7:20)

Adam (a.s.) did not want the *niʿmah* to depart him. So, *Iblis* told him he was not going to live forever wretched, he was not going to live forever alone, he was not going to live forever in sickness and he was not going to live forever decrepit; he would be blessed and it would not depart him if he ate from the forbidden tree. That tipped him over.

The Lesson

What was the ailment in Adam's heart at that moment that *Iblis* leveraged? He had in his heart the longing for foreverness and the wanting to avert any risk that may come.

Social psychologists say that some of the most depressed people are those who are the most risk-averse. Being risk-averse means we are always looking for opportunities, moments and experiences that will not let us down. We do not want to venture, we do not want to experience loss, we do not want to let go of things and we do not want to be in a place where things are uncertain. We are very intentional in trying to control the moment; not only the process, but even the outcome.

It is one thing to say, "I want to be present in the process. I want to be hands-on in the issue. I want to be intentional in the decision-making. I want to be direct in this opportunity and this moment." It is another thing where if we do not achieve what our mind wants, what our heart is intent on and what we strategically plan for, it spins us out of control.

All of us, we have that one friend, one student or one family member who was in love and for whatever reason, it did not work out. For some, it remains a haunting memory that has caused them to miss out on great opportunities that may have arrived to them. It becomes this frozen moment of time that has numbed the rest of their lives. They never find a restart in what could have been a better experience than what they are fixated on in the moment in the past.

It makes sense now when we read this hadith. The Prophet (s.a.w.) said to take advantage of five things before they leave:

> Ibn ʿAbbas reported: The Messenger of Allah (s.a.w.) said, "Take advantage of five before five: your youth before your old age, your health before your illness, your riches before your poverty, your free time before your work, and your life before your death."
>
> (Shuʿab al-Iman lil-Bayhaqi 10250)

Our youth before our old age; our maturity.

Our health before our illness; Allah (s.w.t.) promised us, we will get sick.

Our wealth before loss of wealth; the pain of losing our wealth changes how we look at the world. It is not about we were rich once and later become poor or homeless, but the point is we did not think about the way our finances were—we took it for granted—now they have changed. Everyone will experience this, even Warren Buffett—everyone. Changes occur.

Our free time until we are busy; sometimes we think, "If only I could go back to when I had that little bit more free time. The things I could have done if I just had that little bit more free time." And *subḥānAllāh*, we have a lot of free time. There is a lot of *barakah* in our time.

When my children were in primary school, everything was on auto-pilot—they would come home and do homework. Now, they have soccer training, tutor and many other things—very busy. In the span of only two years, things have changed.

Where are we today compared to where we were before COVID-19? Where were we in COVID-19 in comparison to the year before it? Where are we today in comparison to what we will be in two years, in five years or in ten years? *Wallāhu aʿlam*. All of it—our youth, health, wealth, free time and life—take advantage.

Thus, a lesson from the story of Adam (a.s.): do not be risk-averse, do not be wanting longevity, do not be craving to have the *niʿmah* to the point it cannot depart from us or change to a different way from what we are used to.

Adam (a.s.) was blessed with a different *niʿmah*; the blessing of working for our place in *Jannah* is better than a place in *Jannah* that we did not work for. This is the words of our *ʿulamaʾ*. The blessing of earning our keep is better than to be provided luxury.

Anyone who has had their first job—it does not matter what the first job is—they will feel like they are standing taller when they achieve something. In my first job, I delivered flyers and newspapers. It is a very American and Canadian thing to do.

I was thirteen years old. I told my father that I wanted a job, but he did not want me to work service jobs. I tried to convince him, "My friend is delivering newspapers too. Baba, I can take a round."

"Okay, how many?"

"500 houses a day."

"Oh," my dad said, "Go on then. Let's see. Do you think it will be easy? Go out and see what 500 houses look like."

So I went around delivering newspapers. At house number twenty-five, I was already sweating!

But when I came back home, there was a sense of accomplishment.

To earn our keep is better for us, dear readers. It is a higher regard. Why do we get a higher place in *Jannah* when we have higher *'amal*? Because we have earned it, may Allah (s.w.t.) make us be with the prophets. But we are not going to get there unless we work the way our prophets worked. Did Muḥammad (s.a.w.) work or did he sleep? Did he sleep the whole night or was he awake?

Jannah is not for free—this is the message. If we want it for free, it will bring us ruin. It will bring disharmony to other aspects of our lives.

Hence, the ailment of Adam (a.s.)—the destructive love in this story of Adam (a.s.)—is his desire for eternal happiness, eternal contentment, and to be eternally blessed; to be risk-averse and prone to wanting to shelter ourselves and our families from any exposure to risks, even when the gain could be much greater.

We have, in our culture as Muslims, this statement: *man jadda wajada*. It means the one who ventures with seriousness and deliverance, they will find what they seek. Putting together our intention and trusting Allah (s.w.t.) is the way of Prophet Muḥammad (s.a.w.):

... فَإِذَا عَزَمْتَ فَتَوَكَّلْ عَلَى ٱللَّهِ ۚ إِنَّ
ٱللَّهَ يُحِبُّ ٱلْمُتَوَكِّلِينَ ﴿١٥٩﴾

...And when you have decided, then rely upon Allah. Indeed, Allah loves those who rely [upon Him].

(Surah Ali-'Imran, 3:159)

CHAPTER 8

Love Without Effort

Habil and Qabil

The next story of destructive love is about the first children of Adam (a.s.)—a story about Habil and Qabil.

Qabil was the murderer, the one who desired to have more by doing less. The point of the story of Habil and Qabil is if we are not willing to offer the best of what we have, Allah (s.w.t.) will not accept it as if we have given the best. Allah (s.w.t.) says:

۞وَٱتْلُ عَلَيْهِمْ نَبَأَ ٱبْنَىْ ءَادَمَ بِٱلْحَقِّ
إِذْ قَرَّبَا قُرْبَانًا فَتُقُبِّلَ مِنْ أَحَدِهِمَا وَلَمْ

يُتَقَبَّلْ مِنَ ٱلْآخَرِ قَالَ لَأَقْتُلَنَّكَ ۖ قَالَ
إِنَّمَا يَتَقَبَّلُ ٱللَّهُ مِنَ ٱلْمُتَّقِينَ ﴿٢٧﴾

And recite to them the story of Adam's two sons, in truth, when they both made an offering [to Allah], and it was accepted from one of them but was not accepted from the other. Said [the latter], "I will surely kill you." Said [the former], "Indeed, Allah only accepts from the righteous [who fear Him]."

(Surah al-Ma'idah, 5:27)

Watlu 'alayhim; recite to them. This is a really interesting statement. Who was the Prophet (s.a.w.) ordered to recite this story to? Was it only to the Muslim *ummah*? No. It was also to *Bani Isra'il* because this narrative is also found in the *Tawrah* or Bible. Allah (s.w.t.) was saying to the Prophet (s.a.w.), "Recite it to them, not just to your own people who would believe you, but also to those who have a similar story in their narrative so that they may grow to understand the depth of what We share with them that is hidden from them and has been corrupted, mistranslated and absent from their book. I am going to give you a story that if they were to hear you and listen, they will understand the truthfulness of your claim, Muḥammad."

As Adam (a.s.) began to populate the earth, his wife would give children and they would be a son and daughter—twins. As they grew older, there was a desire for more procreation. What was permitted at that time—to make "genetic diversity" from our scientific words—is that the son born in one pregnancy would marry the daughter born in a different pregnancy. That was the early divergence. It is interesting to note that when geneticists study the human path, they can trace it down to a very small pool of genetics, to one or two genetic origins.

Habil's sister was meant to marry Qabil, while Qabil's sister was meant to marry Habil. Qabil was jealous, "I don't want you to be married to my sister." Adam (a.s.) said, "Allah will decide. Make an oath to Allah and an offering to Allah. Make your *du'a'* to Allah, your *ṣalah* to Allah, and give the best of what you can to Allah and Allah will decide this matter for you."

Allah (s.w.t.) showed His favour by accepting the offering—the giving of *ṣadaqah* to those who were poor—that was done by Habil more so than Qabil. Qabil just took some of his weeds that he had been growing—just a small bundle—and gave it in the way of God, while Habil chose the fattest and the best of his flock to give in the way of Allah (s.w.t.). Therefore, the undoing of Qabil, the destructive love, was that he wanted the best by offering what was least.

High level with low effort was the mentality of Qabil that caused agitation and an impassionate disastrous reaction: Qabil picked up a rock and right after he killed his brother, he became instantaneously *nadim*—regretful. Look at how Allah (s.w.t.) cared. Immediately—before even his brother's soul had departed—the action made him regretful, "I should never have done that. How many words were spoken that I wish I could take back? How many decisions were made that I wish I had thought of first?"

فَبَعَثَ ٱللَّهُ غُرَابًا يَبْحَثُ فِى ٱلْأَرْضِ
لِيُرِيَهُۥ كَيْفَ يُوَٰرِى سَوْءَةَ أَخِيهِ ۚ قَالَ
يَٰوَيْلَتَىٰٓ أَعَجَزْتُ أَنْ أَكُونَ مِثْلَ هَٰذَا

ٱلْغُرَابِ فَأُوَٰرِىَ سَوْءَةَ أَخِى ۖ فَأَصْبَحَ مِنَ ٱلنَّـٰدِمِينَ ﴿٣١﴾

Then Allah sent a crow searching [i.e., scratching] in the ground to show him how to hide the disgrace of his brother. He said, "O' woe to me! Have I failed to be like this crow and hide the disgrace [i.e., body] of my brother?" And he became of the regretful.

(Surah al-Ma'idah, 5:31)

The Lesson

Have you ever had people in your life whose ambition is greater than their output? Have you ever had people who want to be the boss but do not put in the hours, the commitment and the qualification? Have you ever had people who want to take the shortcut, such as taking notes from someone else and misrepresenting it as their own? Allah (s.w.t.) warns against this in the Qur'an:

لَا تَحْسَبَنَّ ٱلَّذِينَ يَفْرَحُونَ بِمَآ أَتَوا
وَّيُحِبُّونَ أَن يُحْمَدُوا بِمَا لَمْ يَفْعَلُوا فَلَا
تَحْسَبَنَّهُم بِمَفَازَةٍ مِّنَ ٱلْعَذَابِ ۖ وَلَهُمْ
عَذَابٌ أَلِيمٌ ١٨٨

And never think that those who rejoice in what they have perpetrated and like to be praised for what they did not do—never think them [to be] in safety from the punishment, and for them is a painful punishment.

(Surah Ali-ʿImran, 3:188)

We will find that a genius in hypocrite loves to be praised and honoured for what they do not perform. They want to be recognised but do not put in the effort, and they will step on others to ascend. This is the mentality of Qabil: the love of more with the commitment of less and the love of wanting to be happy in his home with his wife, but not doing what is necessary.

Whenever I sit between a husband and wife who are aggrieved, they always come prepared. I have never been in a situation where they are not prepared with ammunition. The gun is loaded; the husband would be prepared with points to argue about why his wife is in the wrong, and the wife would also be prepared with her own points. It is very difficult for them to admit that they are a low-level husband or wife. However, when they finally admit it, their lives change.

Life changes when we are willing to accept that we may have not given the best, but we are demanding the best. How can you demand the best when you are giving the worst? When we do not get the best, it then causes anger and resentment. It should really be against ourselves, but it is misdirected to who? To those who are actually giving and doing good.

For example, people try to sabotage others at work. Why do they sabotage someone who is a hard-worker? Sometimes, when people sabotage at work, they are sabotaging someone who is actually a good person, because they are trying to show off and make the good people look bad. This is like Qabil.

What Qabil did is not only murder but it is also a death sentence. It is a death sentence to his family—it ended the life that he had. This is the destructive love of wanting the best without the hard work, at the expense of oneself and others.

CHAPTER 9

Love to Control

Firʿawn and His Rebelling Magicians

These next three chapters will discuss the story of Musa (a.s.). It is an amazing story. May Allah (s.w.t.) allow us to discuss it in depth.

There are five types of people that when they come together, they bring tyranny. Even until our time, when we put together these five characters that Allah (s.w.t.) discusses in the story of Musa (a.s.), we will find corruption and tyranny in the land.

The first of them is Firʿawn. This is the one who wants to rule for themselves, the King or the Queen—whoever who is not leading or ruling to serve their people, to better their lands or to progress their communities, but is leading because they want others to serve them.

Next, the ministers. They are the power behind the power, the one who benefits from who they put on the throne—who takes all of the hate, while they take all of the joy. When Firʿawn wanted a tower to be built, he called upon his trusted minister, "Haman, build something. I want to go up into the heavens, I want to climb up this pyramid. I want to look inside the heavens to see the God of Musa and I think he's lying. There's no one up there."

وَقَالَ فِرْعَوْنُ يَٰهَٰمَٰنُ ٱبْنِ لِى صَرْحًا لَّعَلِّىٓ أَبْلُغُ ٱلْأَسْبَٰبَ ﴿٣٦﴾ أَسْبَٰبَ ٱلسَّمَٰوَٰتِ فَأَطَّلِعَ إِلَىٰٓ إِلَٰهِ مُوسَىٰ وَإِنِّى لَأَظُنُّهُۥ كَٰذِبًا ۚ ... ﴿٣٧﴾

And Firʿawn said, "O' Haman, construct for me a tower that I might reach the ways - The ways into the heavens—so that I may look at the deity of Musa; but indeed, I think he is a liar."...

(Surah Ghafir, 40:36-37)

Haman knew Fir'awn was not going to reach the clouds. He was an engineer so he knew, but he did it anyway. As long as he was happy and wealthy, it was no problem for him. Whatever Fir'awn wanted, Haman gave. He was a corrupt minister who was there to reap the benefits while under the shade of the sovereign.

The third character is the *shurṭah*. They were the police—Fir'awn's army, those who were ordered to crack skulls, break backs and restrain others.

Then, the magicians—the sorcerers. They were people of religion, but crooked. When Fir'awn asked them what he should do to defeat Musa (a.s.), they replied, "Tell all the lands to send their most knowledgeable magicians."

قَالُوٓا۟ أَرْجِهْ وَأَخَاهُ وَأَرْسِلْ فِى ٱلْمَدَآئِنِ حَٰشِرِينَ ﴿١١١﴾ يَأْتُوكَ بِكُلِّ سَٰحِرٍ عَلِيمٍ ﴿١١٢﴾

They said, "Postpone [the matter of] him and his brother and send among the cities gatherers who will bring you every learned magician."

(Surah al-A'raf, 7:111-112)

In this society, they were like the imam or clergy. The *ʿulama'* say that one deviant imam has the power to destroy what a hundred deviant ministers cannot. One deviant religious person can corrupt the religion, the people and their mindset. The magicians were also the media of the time. They broadcasted information from the pulpit, so we can think of them as the spreaders of news of the time. This made them influential in that society.

Finally, the financier, Qarun. He was from the people of Musa (a.s.) and was blessed with wealth from Allah (s.w.t.), but his mindset was, "I have to get paid, I have no obligations to anyone. I'd sell my own family to get rich."

The moment these five characters are put together, they will unjustly govern people in whichever way they want. This is what we can learn from the incredible story of Musa (a.s.).

Our next story of destructive love starts with the magicians. After they faced Musa (a.s.), they immediately entered Islam because they saw what Musa (a.s.) brought was not magic. They knew what they were doing was not real. They were not actually changing their ropes and sticks to actual snakes:

قَالَ بَلْ أَلْقُوا۟ ۖ فَإِذَا حِبَالُهُمْ وَعِصِيُّهُمْ
يُخَيَّلُ إِلَيْهِ مِن سِحْرِهِمْ أَنَّهَا تَسْعَىٰ ﴿٦٦﴾

He said, "Rather, you throw." And suddenly their ropes and staffs seemed to him from their magic that they were moving [like snakes].

(Surah Ṭaha, 20:66)

They only caused an illusion to overcome the gaze of the people. There was no change in the material—but when Musa (a.s.) threw his staff, it became a real snake:

وَأَلْقِ مَا فِى يَمِينِكَ تَلْقَفْ مَا صَنَعُوٓا۟ ۖ
إِنَّمَا صَنَعُوا۟ كَيْدُ سَٰحِرٍ ۖ وَلَا يُفْلِحُ ٱلسَّاحِرُ
حَيْثُ أَتَىٰ ﴿٦٩﴾

And throw what is in your right hand; it will swallow up what they have crafted. What they have crafted is but the trick of a magician, and the magician will not succeed wherever he is.

(Surah Ṭaha, 20:69)

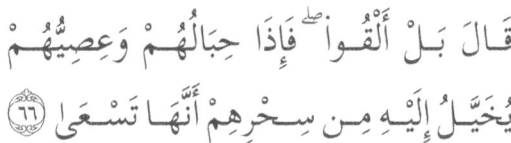

The magicians immediately fell down *sujud*, "Oh no, we're frauds. Musa is real and we are tricksters. Allah is Allah."

فَأُلْقِىَ ٱلسَّحَرَةُ سُجَّدًا قَالُوٓا۟ ءَامَنَّا بِرَبِّ
هَـٰرُونَ وَمُوسَىٰ ﴿٧٠﴾

> So the magicians fell down in prostration. They said, "We have believed in the Lord of Harun and Musa."

(Surah Ṭaha, 20:70)

Firʿawn was embarrassed, but look at this moment of arrogance and control, "Have you believed in him before I gave you permission?"

قَالَ ءَامَنتُمْ لَهُۥ قَبْلَ أَنْ ءَاذَنَ لَكُمْ ۖ إِنَّهُۥ
لَكَبِيرُكُمُ ٱلَّذِى عَلَّمَكُمُ ٱلسِّحْرَ ۖ فَلَأُقَطِّعَنَّ
أَيْدِيَكُمْ وَأَرْجُلَكُم مِّنْ خِلَـٰفٍ وَلَأُصَلِّبَنَّكُمْ
فِى جُذُوعِ ٱلنَّخْلِ وَلَتَعْلَمُنَّ أَيُّنَآ أَشَدُّ عَذَابًا
وَأَبْقَىٰ ﴿٧١﴾

> [Firʿawn] said, "You believed him [i.e., Musa] before I gave you permission. Indeed, he is your leader who has taught you magic. So I will surely cut off your hands and your feet on opposite sides, and I will crucify you on the trunks of palm trees, and you will surely know which of us is more severe in [giving] punishment and more enduring."
>
> (Surah Ṭaha, 20:71)

It is not, "Did you believe in him?" He could clearly see why they believed in Musa (a.s.). Firʿawn knew the truth and this is what made him so destructive; he knew he was wrong but he continued in it. The magicians did not know it was wrong until they saw the outcome. Firʿawn did not ask them, "Are you going to become a believer or not?" Instead, when the magicians fell down *sujud*, he said, "How dare you before I gave you permission?!"

The magicians became martyrs on account of them resisting. They said to Firʿawn, "We prefer the punishment from you in this *dunya* over the punishment from Allah."

قَالُوا۟ لَن نُّؤْثِرَكَ عَلَىٰ مَا جَآءَنَا مِنَ ٱلْبَيِّنَـٰتِ وَٱلَّذِى فَطَرَنَا ۖ فَٱقْضِ مَآ أَنتَ قَاضٍ ۖ إِنَّمَا تَقْضِى هَـٰذِهِ ٱلْحَيَوٰةَ ٱلدُّنْيَآ ﴿٧٢﴾

They said, "Never will we prefer you over what has come to us of clear proofs and [over] He who created us. So decree whatever you are to decree. You can only decree for this worldly life."

(Surah Ṭaha, 20:72)

It is important to note that the magicians actually had not heard much from Musa (a.s.) yet. They just saw the truth, they felt it in their hearts, and immediately became willing to die for it.

The Lesson

Putting ourselves between other people's conscience is never meant to be a place for us, the created. Putting ourselves in a place where we do not give people the ability to make decisions about even their own *iman*, is never meant to be the way in the sunnah of the Prophet Muḥammad (s.a.w.). Allah (s.w.t.) says, "Let the one who wants to come to faith, believe."

...فَمَن شَآءَ فَلْيُؤْمِن... ﴿٢٩﴾

...so whoever wills—let him believe...

(Surah al-Kahf, 18:29)

Those who want to control and dominate others cannot see this and therefore, the love of being the one who dictates other people in every aspect of their life is a sinful destructive love. The love of commanding others, even if it is for righteous things, is destructive.

As a father, I have nurtured my children to pray because Allah (s.w.t.) instructs us to pray, not to pray because I have taught them to pray. There is a big difference between the two. If I come home and ask my son, "Have you prayed *'Aṣr* yet?" This question has the right intention, but it is asked in the wrong way.

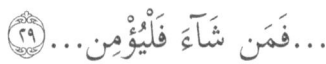

When we show that our command is not the command of Allah (s.w.t.) but it is our command, then when our child gets to an age where they fear our reaction—overreaction—this can lead to the consequence of them not admitting their *ṣalah* has not been maintained. We may have lost them for life when this happens.

For example, if my son says he has not prayed *ʿAṣr* yet and I get furious, yelling at him, he will become more fearful of admitting the truth. He will lie the next time, saying he has prayed or will pray soon, but carry on playing on his phone and such. It is rare for kids to correct it in their room.

It is better to say, "I haven't prayed *ʿAṣr* yet. Do you want to pray with me?" It is better when we set a schedule in our home of who will be the imam for *Maghrib* or who will be the imam for *ʿIshaʾ*. It is better when we appoint a *muʾadhdhin* and another one to make *iqamah*. It is better when we have a standardised time for the *ṣalah*, that even if our kids are doing their homework, they should take a break for five minutes to pray.

We should exclude our authoritarianism in the routine of *ṣalah*. There is a difference between being an authoritarian, which is being pharaonic in our command; and being someone who is authoritative, someone who is leading by example. The latter is where we seek to go.

If we can implement in our children that the truth is dearer than the command of the truth, they will feel their connection to Allah (s.w.t.) as being more important than pleasing us, that they can actually take comfort in admitting to us, "No, I have not prayed, but *inshā'Allāh*, I will. I know what I need to do."

Then, we have to back up, back away. The *ṣalah* is between them and Allah (s.w.t.). We should know that our children have the ability to contradict us in a way that is pleasing to Allah (s.w.t.). It is the greatest of ways that we can nurture them.

CHAPTER 10

Love of Conflict

The Drowning of Fir'awn

At one point in the story of Musa (a.s.), he was brought by Allah's order to the edge of a sea, fleeing from Fir'awn and his army. At that moment, the people of *Bani Isra'il* who were quick to forget Allah (s.w.t.), quick to relinquish their faith, quick to panic, quick to lose their *ṣabr*, and quick to forget *tawakkul*, they said, "What have you done to us, Musa? Now we're destroyed. You brought us with no strategic advantage, escape or retreat. Fir'awn is coming. He's going to capture us and put us to death."

فَلَمَّا تَرَٰٓءَا ٱلْجَمْعَانِ قَالَ أَصْحَٰبُ مُوسَىٰٓ إِنَّا لَمُدْرَكُونَ ﴿٦١﴾

And when the two companies saw one another, the companions of Musa said, "Indeed, we are to be overtaken!"

(Surah ash-Shu'ara', 26:61)

Musa (a.s.) replied, "Never. Allah is with me."

قَالَ كَلَّآ ۖ إِنَّ مَعِىَ رَبِّى سَيَهْدِينِ ﴿٦٢﴾

[Musa] said, "No! Indeed, with me is my Lord; He will guide me."

(Surah ash-Shu'ara', 26:62)

He did not say, "Allah is with us," because they gave up. He was saying, "Allah is with me even if you give up." Then, Allah (s.w.t.) sent the angel Jibril (a.s.) to assist Musa (a.s.) and Allah (s.w.t.) told him, "Hit the water, it will part. It will make a passageway."

فَأَوْحَيْنَآ إِلَىٰ مُوسَىٰٓ أَنِ ٱضْرِب بِّعَصَاكَ ٱلْبَحْرَ ۖ فَٱنفَلَقَ فَكَانَ كُلُّ فِرْقٍ كَٱلطَّوْدِ ٱلْعَظِيمِ ﴿٦٣﴾

Then We inspired to Musa, "Strike with your staff the sea," and it parted, and each portion was like a great towering mountain.

(Surah ash-Shu'ara', 26:63)

Jibril (a.s.) descended in the form of a man and crossed the sea. *Bani Isra'il* followed after him and right after Musa (a.s.) had crossed, he turned around with his staff. He was about to strike the sea again to bring it back together, because he saw Fir'awn and his troops were about to cross.

I want you to think of this moment. Could you imagine if you were in the army of Fir'awn? Imagine you were standing and you saw the sea was parted like mountains. Look at the arrogance and the blindness of Fir'awn.

If I were Fir'awn—*alḥamdulillāh* I am not—I would turn to my people and say, "See? I have kept them out and Egypt is free. I got rid of them. Let's go back. I am still Firʿawn and I am the winner. I still have my army and my country." But this is not what he did.

Arrogance. He was too arrogant to turn back.

So, Musa (a.s.) was holding his staff and about to strike the sea again, but Allah (s.w.t.) said, "Musa, leave the water alone."

وَٱتْرُكِ ٱلْبَحْرَ رَهْوًا ۖ إِنَّهُمْ جُندٌ مُّغْرَقُونَ ٢٤

"And leave the sea in stillness. Indeed, they are an army to be drowned."

(Surah ad-Dukhan, 44:24)

Firʿawn and his soldiers continued to chase after Musa (a.s.). They did not stop. He and his followers, all of them were in error:

...إِنَّ فِرْعَوْنَ وَهَٰمَٰنَ وَجُنُودَهُمَا كَانُوا۟ خَٰطِـِٔينَ ٨

> ...Indeed, Firʿawn and Haman and their soldiers were deliberate sinners.
>
> (Surah al-Qaṣaṣ, 28:8)

As they were crossing the parted sea, Allah (s.w.t.) drowned them but He said Firʿawn was to blame:

فَأَخَذْنَٰهُ وَجُنُودَهُۥ فَنَبَذْنَٰهُمْ فِى ٱلْيَمِّ وَهُوَ مُلِيمٌ ﴿٤٠﴾

> So We took him and his soldiers and cast them into the sea, and he was blameworthy.
>
> (Surah adh-Dhariyat, 51:40)

Firʿawn saw the sea parted like mountains but he still crossed. Allah (s.w.t.) drowned him but the blame was his. He took a step forward, when he should have taken a step back. He committed himself to violence when he should have wanted peace.

The Lesson

Sometimes, we stand at the edge of a problem. If only we would just back away and let it go, if we do not need to have the last word in an argument, if we would just stop blaming others, if we would just be quiet, and if we would just turn around. Just step back from the brink, do not step forward.

There are some of us who ask, why did Allah do this to me? You came to the edge but you did not want to stop. Firʿawn was at the edge but he persisted. His love of hate—of violence, of conflict—pushed him off the edge. He wanted to prove that he was right even when he knew he was wrong, he wanted to prove Musa (a.s.) was wrong even when he knew Musa (a.s.) was right. He was blinded.

People can get so blinded with rage and anger, blinded with their want of revenge. I am not saying we have to step back only when we are wrong. We have to step back from the edge even when we are right. Sometimes, it is a lose-lose situation, even when we should be the winner.

How many of us say something that we regret after? I got a message from a sister the other day. She said, "Shaykh, I've been married for fourteen months.

I made a mistake. I was upset with my husband and said things to him in front of his mother that I shouldn't. I was angry. I regret it from the depths of my heart. He hasn't seen me for four weeks now."

Sometimes, we say something without thinking, but words cannot be taken back. Just like Firʿawn, we cannot swim back—we will not make it back to shore.

Impatience causes this to happen. The love of wanting to have the last word, the love of wanting to prove our point, and the love of being right. Some things we can think about, but are not worthy of mention.

CHAPTER 11

Love That is Misguided

The Samiri and the Golden Calf

The story of the Samiri is like a side story to the story of Musa (a.s.). He was from a tribe of *Bani Israʾīl.* He saw Jibril (a.s.) while they were crossing the parted sea and he saw Jibril's footprint in the sand. He was in awe; he took the dirt from the footprint of Jibril (a.s.) and put it in a bag. Musa (a.s.) was not aware of this.

After they had safely crossed to the other side of the sea, Musa (a.s.) said to Harun (a.s.), "You stay with them. I want to hurry to Allah, I want to go to the mountain, I want to receive the *Tawrah.* Follow my path and you'll find your way in the desert up to the mountain."

...وَقَالَ مُوسَىٰ لِأَخِيهِ هَٰرُونَ ٱخْلُفْنِى فِى قَوْمِى وَأَصْلِحْ وَلَا تَتَّبِعْ سَبِيلَ ٱلْمُفْسِدِينَ ﴿١٤٢﴾

...And Musa said to his brother Harun, "Take my place among my people, do right [by them], and do not follow the way of the corrupters."

(Surah al-A'raf, 7:142)

When Musa (a.s.) arrived, standing on the mountain, Allah (s.w.t.) asked him, "Musa, why did you leave your people behind in a hurry?"

۞ وَمَآ أَعْجَلَكَ عَن قَوْمِكَ يَٰمُوسَىٰ ﴿٨٣﴾

[Allah said], "And what made you hasten from your people, O' Musa?"

(Surah Ṭaha, 20:83)

Musa (a.s.) replied, "O' Allah, they're coming. They're following the footsteps that I laid. They will catch up soon and O' Allah, I came to please you."

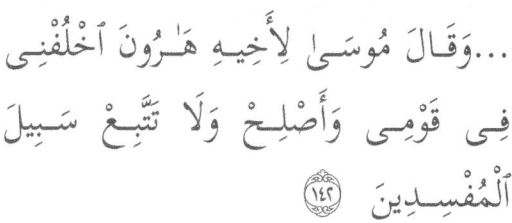

قَالَ هُمْ أُولَآءِ عَلَىٰٓ أَثَرِى وَعَجِلْتُ إِلَيْكَ رَبِّ لِتَرْضَىٰ ﴿٨٤﴾

He said, "They are close upon my tracks, and I hastened to You, my Lord, that You be pleased."

(Surah Ṭaha, 20:84)

Then, Allah (s.w.t.) told him, "Go back. I have tested your people and they failed. The Samiri misguided them with the test I gave them."

قَالَ فَإِنَّا قَدْ فَتَنَّا قَوْمَكَ مِنۢ بَعْدِكَ وَأَضَلَّهُمُ ٱلسَّامِرِىُّ ﴿٨٥﴾

[Allah] said, "But indeed, We have tried your people after you [departed], and the Samiri has led them astray."

(Surah Ṭaha, 20:85)

Musa (a.s.) was shocked, "*SubḥānAllāh*, it has not even been that long. Allah saved us, but they're worshipping a golden calf? How?" *Bid'ah*. This is the danger of *bid'ah*. How did *bid'ah* start amongst them?

Musa (a.s.) returned and in anger, he said to his people:

فَرَجَعَ مُوسَىٰٓ إِلَىٰ قَوْمِهِۦ غَضْبَٰنَ أَسِفًا ۚ قَالَ يَٰقَوْمِ أَلَمْ يَعِدْكُمْ رَبُّكُمْ وَعْدًا حَسَنًا ۚ أَفَطَالَ عَلَيْكُمُ ٱلْعَهْدُ أَمْ أَرَدتُّمْ أَن يَحِلَّ عَلَيْكُمْ غَضَبٌ مِّن رَّبِّكُمْ فَأَخْلَفْتُم مَّوْعِدِى ﴿٨٦﴾

So Musa returned to his people, angry and grieved. He said, "O' my people, did your Lord not make you a good promise? Then, was the time [of its fulfilment] too long for you, or did you wish that wrath from your Lord descend upon you, so you broke your promise [of obedience] to me?"

(Surah Ṭaha, 20:86)

His people who followed the lead of the Samiri replied:

قَالُوا۟ مَآ أَخْلَفْنَا مَوْعِدَكَ بِمَلْكِنَا وَلَـٰكِنَّا
حُمِّلْنَآ أَوْزَارًا مِّن زِينَةِ ٱلْقَوْمِ فَقَذَفْنَـٰهَا
فَكَذَٰلِكَ أَلْقَى ٱلسَّامِرِىُّ ﴿٨٧﴾ فَأَخْرَجَ
لَهُمْ عِجْلًا جَسَدًا لَّهُۥ خُوَارٌ فَقَالُوا۟ هَـٰذَآ
إِلَـٰهُكُمْ وَإِلَـٰهُ مُوسَىٰ فَنَسِىَ ﴿٨٨﴾

They said, "We did not break our promise to you by our will, but we were made to carry burdens from the ornaments of the people [of Fir'awn], so we threw them [into the fire], and thus did the Samiri throw." And he extracted for them [the statue of] a calf which had a lowing sound, and they said, "This is your god and the god of Musa, but he forgot."

(Surah Ṭaha, 20:87-88)

Who exactly was the Samiri? Why were they listening to this ignorant person? Many of us listen to ignorant people, is this not right?

Then, Musa (a.s.) seized his brother by his beard and head:

... وَأَلْقَى ٱلْأَلْوَاحَ وَأَخَذَ بِرَأْسِ أَخِيهِ يَجُرُّهُۥٓ إِلَيْهِ ۚ ... ﴿١٥٠﴾

...And he threw down the tablets and seized his brother by [the hair of] his head, pulling him toward him...

(Surah al-Aʿraf, 7:150)

He said, "What did you do? I left you behind only for a short time. You couldn't keep them in order? They're worshipping an idol?"

قَالَ يَٰهَٰرُونُ مَا مَنَعَكَ إِذْ رَأَيْتَهُمْ ضَلُّوٓا۟ ﴿٩٢﴾ أَلَّا تَتَّبِعَنِ ۖ أَفَعَصَيْتَ أَمْرِى ﴿٩٣﴾

[Musa] said, "O' Harun, what prevented you, when you saw them going astray, from following me? Then have you disobeyed my order?"

(Surah Ṭaha, 20:92-93)

Harun (a.s.) replied, "O' son of my mother, let go of my beard. Let go of my head. They would not listen."

قَالَ يَبْنَؤُمَّ لَا تَأْخُذْ بِلِحْيَتِى وَلَا بِرَأْسِىٓ ۖ إِنِّى خَشِيتُ أَن تَقُولَ فَرَّقْتَ بَيْنَ بَنِىٓ إِسْرَٰٓءِيلَ وَلَمْ تَرْقُبْ قَوْلِى ﴿٩٤﴾

[Harun] said, "O' son of my mother, do not seize [me] by my beard or by my head. Indeed, I feared that you would say, 'You caused division among the Children of Isra'il, and you did not observe [or await] my word.'"

(Surah Ṭaha, 20:94)

After that, Musa (a.s.) asked the Samiri:

قَالَ فَمَا خَطْبُكَ يَٰسَٰمِرِىُّ ﴿٩٥﴾

[Musa] said, "And what is your case, O' Samiri?"

(Surah Ṭaha, 20:95)

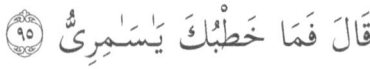

The Samiri replied, "The messenger who came down from God to lead us to safety, I took the sand from his *athar* and placed it in the fire. I melted it and I created for the people something. The messenger is from Allah, so I want to give the people something holy. I want to use something that is good and blessed."

قَالَ بَصُرْتُ بِمَا لَمْ يَبْصُرُوا۟ بِهِۦ فَقَبَضْتُ
قَبْضَةً مِّنْ أَثَرِ ٱلرَّسُولِ فَنَبَذْتُهَا وَكَذَٰلِكَ
سَوَّلَتْ لِى نَفْسِى ﴿٩٦﴾

He said, "I saw what they did not see, so I took a handful [of dust] from the track of the messenger and threw it, and thus did my soul entice me."

(Surah Ṭaha, 20:96)

The Lesson

The basis of *bid'ah* is anything in religion that looks like it is part of the religion, but it is actually not. It may sound like *dhikr*, *tasbiḥ*, or *tahlil*, but it is not from the sunnah of the Prophet (s.a.w.).

Let me share with you a story about this one brother who came with me to *'umrah*. May Allah (s.w.t.) forgive the brother. He loves Muḥammad (s.a.w.), but *bid'ah* is not sunnah. We cannot love the Prophet (s.a.w.) but do *bid'ah*.

We were in Uḥud. I like to get the people following me to take their shoes off and to walk on the sand of Uḥud, to feel it. I told them about the buildings and where Ḥamzah (r.a.) passed away and was first buried.

The brother was awestruck. May Allah (s.w.t.) forgive us and him.

He was sitting on the ground on the mountain. He took some of the dust and swallowed it. I said, "*Lā 'ilāha 'illa-llāh. Allāhu Akbar*, what are you doing, brother?" He said, "Shaykh, I love this."

It was next-level *bid'ah*, out of this world!

I told him, "No, brother. You are going to go to the hospital. Don't do this." He was an elder brother, beautiful brother. May Allah (s.w.t.) grant him *khayr*.

Hence, we learn from this that *bid'ah* always has a religious good intention. I want you to remember this: the basis of *bid'ah* is a person who loves Allah (s.w.t.) and His Prophet Muḥammad (s.a.w.), but it is not the path of the sunnah. It is from a good place in their mind, something they believe is good, but it is not the path of the Prophet Muḥammad (s.a.w.).

If someone tells us to read surah al-Ikhlaṣ 10,000 times for us to get married, this is *bid'ah*. What if we read it 9,999 times? What if we have lost count? They will tell us that we have to start from the beginning.

Bid'ah looks like a part of the religion because of that. It is a good deed to read the Qur'an, but the Prophet Muḥammad (s.a.w.) never told us to do a deed 10,000 times. There is no *du'a'* of the Prophet (s.a.w.) that ever exceeds over one hundred. In all of the sunnah, he never said to do anything more than one hundred except he said:

Ibn 'Umar narrated that one day:

> The Messenger of Allah (s.a.w.) said to his Companions: "Say, 'Glory is to Allah and with His Praise (*SubḥānAllāh, wa biḥamdih*),' a hundred times. Whoever says [it] one time, it

> is written for him ten, and whoever says it ten (times), it is written for him a hundred, and whoever says it a hundred (times), it is written for him a thousand, and whoever increases, Allah will increase for him, and whoever seeks Allah's forgiveness, [Allah] will forgive him."
>
> (Jamiʿ at-Tirmidhi 3470)

He would never burden us.

In one Ramadan, Prophet Muḥammad (s.a.w.) led *ṣalah* for a few nights in a mosque. Then, on the third and fourth nights, he (s.a.w.) stopped. He (s.a.w.) felt it was too much for his *ummah*:

Narrated ʿA'ishah the mother of the faithful believers:

> One night Allah's Messenger (s.a.w.) offered the prayer in the Mosque and the people followed him. The next night he also offered the prayer and too many people gathered. On the third and the fourth nights more people gathered, but Allah's Messenger (s.a.w.) did not come out to them. In the morning he said, "I saw what you were doing and nothing but the fear that it (i.e.

> the prayer) might be enjoined on you, stopped me from coming to you." And that happened in the month of Ramadan.
>
> (Ṣaḥiḥ al-Bukhari 1129)

In our present time, we have ignorant people who tell us to do things that are beyond our abilities, tell us to give more than what we can give and say more than what we can say—not from the sunnah of the Prophet (s.a.w.). This is the misguided love for Allah (s.w.t.) and His Prophet (s.a.w.)—a blind love that leads to *bid'ah* that is not sanctioned, allowed, taught or expected in the teachings of our Prophet Muḥammad (s.a.w.). May Allah (s.w.t.) grant us a love for the sunnah and a love for the simple way of the Prophet (s.a.w.).

This handful of dust by the Samiri becomes a symbol in the Qur'an that if someone loves the way of the Prophet (s.a.w.) and loves the way of Allah (s.w.t.), its measure is not the love in their emotion. Its measure is the love in their practice of the sunnah:

قُلْ إِن كُنتُمْ تُحِبُّونَ ٱللَّهَ فَٱتَّبِعُونِى
يُحْبِبْكُمُ ٱللَّهُ وَيَغْفِرْ لَكُمْ ذُنُوبَكُمْ ۗ وَٱللَّهُ
غَفُورٌ رَّحِيمٌ ﴿٣١﴾

Say, [O' Muḥammad], "If you should love Allah, then follow me, [so] Allah will love you and forgive you your sins. And Allah is Forgiving and Merciful."

(Surah Ali-'Imran, 3:31)

CHAPTER 12

Love of *Kufr*

The Farmer who Forgot Allah (s.w.t.)

In surah al-Kahf, there is a story about two farmers who had neighbouring estates. Both of them irrigated their farms from similar wells and river, and used the same farming techniques and the same seeds.

The first farmer's garden was thriving, whereas the garden of his neighbour was not as lush and productive despite working just as hard—there was barely any profit.

The first farmer entered his garden and he was impressed with himself. He said to his neighbour in arrogance and pride, "I have put in the energy and techniques for agriculture. This is all my doing."

وَكَانَ لَهُۥ ثَمَرٌ فَقَالَ لِصَٰحِبِهِۦ وَهُوَ
يُحَاوِرُهُۥٓ أَنَا۠ أَكْثَرُ مِنكَ مَالًا وَأَعَزُّ نَفَرًا
﴿٣٤﴾ وَدَخَلَ جَنَّتَهُۥ وَهُوَ ظَالِمٌ لِّنَفْسِهِۦ
قَالَ مَآ أَظُنُّ أَن تَبِيدَ هَٰذِهِۦٓ أَبَدًا ﴿٣٥﴾
وَمَآ أَظُنُّ ٱلسَّاعَةَ قَآئِمَةً وَلَئِن رُّدِدتُّ إِلَىٰ
رَبِّى لَأَجِدَنَّ خَيْرًا مِّنْهَا مُنقَلَبًا ﴿٣٦﴾

And he had fruit, so he said to his companion while he was conversing with him, "I am greater than you in wealth and mightier in [numbers of] men." And he entered his garden while he was unjust to himself. He said, "I do not think that this will perish—ever. And I do not think the Hour will occur. And even if I should be brought back to my Lord, I will surely find better than this as a return."

(Surah al-Kahf, 18:34-36)

He entered his garden while wronging himself because his mindset was wrong—he was not grateful to Allah (s.w.t.). He was thinking, "I cannot ever imagine that anything could happen to this garden of mine. Its roots are deep. Its stem and trunk of the trees are strong. Its yearly production has a precedent of thriving and profitability. What could change?"

His neighbour said, "This is a blessing. I'm happy for you, but remember that all of us have challenges. All of us will be standing in front of Allah. Perhaps you need to consider that you will be held accountable for these words you just said. Don't put yourself at a place above Allah. If you were to look at me, I have done what you've done. Although I have not been as prosperous as you, I remain thankful to Allah."

قَالَ لَهُۥ صَاحِبُهُۥ وَهُوَ يُحَاوِرُهُۥٓ أَكَفَرْتَ
بِٱلَّذِى خَلَقَكَ مِن تُرَابٍ ثُمَّ مِن نُّطْفَةٍ
ثُمَّ سَوَّىٰكَ رَجُلًا ٣٧ لَّٰكِنَّا۠ هُوَ ٱللَّهُ رَبِّى
وَلَآ أُشْرِكُ بِرَبِّىٓ أَحَدًا ٣٨ وَلَوْلَآ إِذْ
دَخَلْتَ جَنَّتَكَ قُلْتَ مَا شَآءَ ٱللَّهُ لَا قُوَّةَ
إِلَّا بِٱللَّهِ ۚ ... ٣٩

> His companion said to him while he was conversing with him, "Have you disbelieved in He who created you from dust and then from a sperm-drop and then proportioned you [as] a man? But as for me, He is Allah, my Lord, and I do not associate with my Lord anyone. And why did you, when you entered your garden, not say, 'What Allah willed [has occurred]; there is no power except in Allah?'" …
>
> (Surah al-Kahf, 18:37-39)

Then, Allah (s.w.t.) caused—in the span of a short period of time—the first farmer's land to change. His wells began to dry, fungal infection began to overcome his fruits, and birds began to prey on his land and yield. On the other hand, his neighbour's land was protected, even though he had not added or changed anything.

The first farmer woke up to the disaster looming at his farm. He was struck with distress that he was clasping his hands together in regret. He said to himself, "I wish I had not made *shirk* with Allah."

وَأُحِيطَ بِثَمَرِهِۦ فَأَصْبَحَ يُقَلِّبُ كَفَّيْهِ عَلَىٰ
مَآ أَنفَقَ فِيهَا وَهِىَ خَاوِيَةٌ عَلَىٰ عُرُوشِهَا
وَيَقُولُ يَٰلَيْتَنِى لَمْ أُشْرِكْ بِرَبِّىٓ أَحَدًا ﴿٤٢﴾

And his fruits were encompassed [by ruin], so he began to turn his hands about [in dismay] over what he had spent on it, while it had collapsed upon its trellises, and said, "Oh, I wish I had not associated with my Lord anyone."

(Surah al-Kahf, 18:42)

The Lesson

Sometimes, we look at our fortune in life and we assume that our education, our family name or the status that we have today is our doing or it is because we are worthy of it. We assume that the reason some people do not have what we have is because they do not have the right mindset.

Now, the point is not that the mindset is not important. The Prophet (s.a.w.) was very optimistic, positive and financially savvy, so that is not the point here. Instead, it is not only the mindset. It is also genetics and the things we have been blessed and provided with by Allah (s.w.t.) that we have no control over.

For example, I will never have a son or daughter who is like Michael Phelps, the American swimmer. His armspan is abnormal for a human being, the length of his arms and the reach that he has. I can try throwing my son in a pool 30 hours a day—forget 24 hours—but he will still never be Michael Phelps. We should acknowledge that the blessings that we have are from Allah (s.w.t.).

There is a wonderful book by Malcom Gladwell called "Outliers". He did statistical analysis of why certain people are in a place where they are. Do you think Bill Gates is so much smarter than everyone in the world that he could be the only one who could start Microsoft? No. Did you know that Bill Gates' next-door neighbour was a computer scientist and professor at Massachusetts Institute of Technology (MIT)?

When he was eleven years old, his mother asked their neighbour, "Hey, my son's really interested in computers. Can he come and hang out in your lab?" This was in the 1970s. This privileged and wealthy young man at eleven years old was in an MIT computer lab when computers only existed in six universities in America. He was in a lab where even PhD students could only sit in it once a semester. He was there daily.

Another example we can look at is Steve Jobs. In an interview, he said he called up Hewlett-Packard—not the company but one of the founders himself, Bill Hewlett—because he wanted some computer parts. Bill Hewlett was amused and offered Steve Jobs an internship at his company, so Steve Jobs worked on Hewlett-Packard's assembly line, assembling computers as a teenager.

The opening that Allah (s.w.t.) provides and to whom He provides. It is not just our effort, thinking that we are smarter than others or working harder than others, thinking that others are not in the same place as us because they are not smart enough or not working hard enough. It is all from Allah (s.w.t.).

Therefore, I end this chapter with this concept: one of the destructive elements of love is when we look at ourselves as self-made and forget to show gratitude to Allah (s.w.t.).

CHAPTER 13

Love of Defiance

The Sabbath Fishermen

There was once a community of fishermen from *Bani Isra'il* who thought they were smart enough to trick Allah (s.w.t.) to circumvent His violation. Allah (s.w.t.) prohibited them to work on the day of Sabbath on every Saturday as it was a day of reflection and worship. Then, they were tested by Allah (s.w.t.):

وَسْـَٔلْهُمْ عَنِ ٱلْقَرْيَةِ ٱلَّتِى كَانَتْ حَاضِرَةَ
ٱلْبَحْرِ إِذْ يَعْدُونَ فِى ٱلسَّبْتِ إِذْ تَأْتِيهِمْ
حِيتَانُهُمْ يَوْمَ سَبْتِهِمْ شُرَّعًا وَيَوْمَ لَا

يَسْبِتُونَ ۙ لَا تَأْتِيهِمْ ۚ كَذَٰلِكَ نَبْلُوهُم بِمَا
كَانُوا يَفْسُقُونَ ﴿١٦٣﴾

And ask them about the town that was by the sea—when they transgressed in [the matter of] the Sabbath—when their fish came to them openly on their Sabbath day, and the day they had no Sabbath they did not come to them. Thus did We give them trial because they were defiantly disobedient.

(Surah al-Aʿraf, 7:163)

The fish would only swim close to the surface of the water on Saturdays when the fishermen were prohibited to catch them. On other days, the fish would be hidden from them.

What they did to circumvent Allah's violation was they put their nets out on Friday and collected the fish on Sunday. They thought if they did not touch the net on Saturday, it would not be a violation of Allah's command. They thought they were smarter than the laws of Allah (s.w.t.), so He cursed them for it and they became apes:

فَلَمَّا عَتَوْا۟ عَن مَّا نُهُوا۟ عَنْهُ قُلْنَا لَهُمْ
كُونُوا۟ قِرَدَةً خَـٰسِـِٔينَ ﴿١٦٦﴾

So when they were insolent about that which they had been forbidden, We said to them, "Be apes, despised."

(Surah al-Aʿraf, 7:166)

What is the curse of *Bani Isra'il*? Their curse is although they know what the truth is, they do not completely follow it. There will always be light missing from their path.

The Lesson

Sometimes, there are people who would come to me and their question would start with, "Shaykh, what if?"

Don't.

With Allah (s.w.t.), be careful. With Allah (s.w.t.), we do not want to be in the territory of being imaginative. Do not be too smart, do not play with Allah's commands, do not play with His *deen*, and do not be inventive with the *shari'ah*.

There is right and wrong, not just better and worse. Some things, there is no flexibility, so do not try to circumvent Allah (s.w.t.). He says, "They were planning, but Allah's plan is more complete."

...وَيَمْكُرُونَ وَيَمْكُرُ ٱللَّهُ ۖ وَٱللَّهُ خَيْرُ ٱلْمَٰكِرِينَ ﴿٣٠﴾

...But they plan, and Allah plans. And Allah is the best of planners.

(Surah al-Anfal, 8:30)

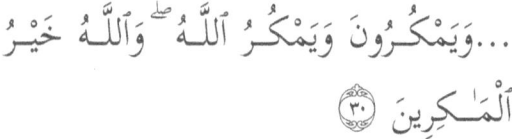

CHAPTER 14

Love Without Restraint

The People of Luṭ (a.s.)

The final destructive love that we want to discuss is the love of the flesh, the love of desire, and the love of promiscuity. There is a lesson in our revulsion of sexual immorality and deviant practices.

We can take the story of the people of Luṭ (a.s.) as an example. It is a prominent story in the Qur'an. What made the people of Luṭ (a.s.) the people of lewd is that they said, "We hear and we disobey. We do what we want."

...سَمِعْنَا وَعَصَيْنَا... ﴿٤٦﴾

..."We hear and disobey"...

(Surah an-Nisa', 4:46)

Luṭ (a.s.) said to his people, "If only I had the strength to help you and to change you, if only I had the strength to stop you, or I could find strength from other than myself."

قَالَ لَوْ أَنَّ لِى بِكُمْ قُوَّةً أَوْ ءَاوِىٓ إِلَىٰ رُكْنٍ شَدِيدٍ ﴿٨٠﴾

He said, "If only I had against you some power or could take refuge in a strong support."

(Surah Hud, 11:80)

What destroyed the people of Luṭ (a.s.), the cities of Sodom and Gomorrah? They changed things upside down. They perverted themselves upside down, so the punishment that they received is:

فَلَمَّا جَآءَ أَمْرُنَا جَعَلْنَا عَـٰلِيَهَا سَافِلَهَا وَأَمْطَرْنَا عَلَيْهَا حِجَارَةً مِّن سِجِّيلٍ مَّنضُودٍ ﴿٨٢﴾

So when Our command came, We made the highest part [of the city] its lowest and rained upon them stones of layered hard clay, [which were]

(Surah Hud, 11:82)

The wife of Luṭ (a.s.) was also punished because although she did not practise lewdness, she accepted it. What brought the wife of Luṭ (a.s.) out of the mercy of Allah (s.w.t.) was that she was accepting of what she knew was not right, not that she practised what was wrong:

فَأَنجَيْنَـٰهُ وَأَهْلَهُۥٓ إِلَّا ٱمْرَأَتَهُۥ كَانَتْ مِنَ ٱلْغَـٰبِرِينَ ﴿٨٣﴾

> So We saved him and his family, except for his wife; she was of those who remained [with the evildoers].
>
> (Surah al-A'raf, 7:83)

This becomes an important lesson within our hearts as Muslims.

The Lesson

There are those who might say, "Love is love," but it is not. Love is what is pure. Love is not what is opposite to the truth and opposite to the mandate of Allah (s.w.t.) for humanity—love is not what is haram.

Therefore, this story is about the love of the flesh, the love of fulfilling desires, the love of breaking the boundaries, the love of going beyond the limits of halal, the love of stepping outside one's marriage, even if it is not physical. Even with just the sight; the epidemic of pornography.

Did you know the average age for a child in Australia to be exposed to explicit sexual content is ten years old? By the age of ten, 96% have viewed something explicit. It is not that they search for it, it just happens because someone would show it to them and they would watch it. The age of ten is the average age. May Allah (s.w.t.) protect our homes and children. The love of the perverse is meant to be countered by the teachings, the hadith and the sunnah of our Prophet Muḥammad (s.a.w.). All of us—as individuals, families, communities, societies, countries and regions—have to learn about what destroyed the nations before us.

We live in a time today where it is difficult in certain places in the world to speak openly about what was common sense in the past. Things that relate to gender, questions like 'what is a man?' and 'what is a woman?' It seems very easy. A man is a man, a woman is a woman. In certain places, this is not as straightforward. Some people want others to call them by what they want to be called, not as what they are. And by law, they want that right. These are the things that are being debated and combated in many Western countries.

The love of the excess, the love of the immediacy of what one feels. It is not about the perverseness of the sexual attitude. What drives it is the love of making our own choice, as if we do not have a master, do not have *Rabb*, do not have *Ilah*, and do not have *Malik*. Look at some of the last verses in the Qur'an:

قُلْ أَعُوذُ بِرَبِّ ٱلنَّاسِ ﴿١﴾ مَلِكِ ٱلنَّاسِ ﴿٢﴾ إِلَٰهِ ٱلنَّاسِ ﴿٣﴾

Say, "I seek refuge in the Lord of mankind, the Sovereign of mankind, the God of mankind."

(Surah an-Nas, 114:1-3)

Mankind, we have a *Rabb*, we have a Master. He is the One we should devote ourselves to and obey. He is the King of our lives, the One who says right is right, wrong is wrong, halal is halal, and haram is haram, even if we feel differently.

A healthy man or a healthy woman may have a natural attraction to someone else who is haram for them to marry. However, just because we have this natural attraction, it does not mean we can step outside of what is halal. Just because we feel it, it does not mean we are to do it—this is an important perspective. If we allow it, this feeling will then control the mind and emotions, part of the soul. When the soul is no longer pure, when the soul is no longer intact, and when the soul is no longer healed, then it leaves the body to say, "I can do whatever I want. I only live once. I only have one opportunity. If I do not do it now, when will I do it? I'm too young, my time will be over." This becomes the most important marketing strategy that is used against us as human beings. A machinery of deception to make alluring that which has always been seen as repugnant.

The destructive love is that a person believes they are entitled to do whatever they feel is right. We are not meant to live in a life where we do whatever we feel is right. That is why the greatest title of Prophet Muḥammad (s.a.w.) is "*ʿAbdullah*", the slave of Allah (s.w.t.).

Why do you give your son the name ʿAbdullah? What is your hope? The hope is so that your son will be a slave to the order of Allah (s.w.t.). When Allah (s.w.t.) says stand, he will stand; *sujud*, he will make *sujud*; give *zakah* from his hard-earned money, he will give; do not drink water during Ramadan, he will not drink despite how hot it is.

Now, let us look at the hadith of the Prophet Muḥammad (s.a.w.).

Abu Saʿid said:

> "I heard the Messenger of Allah (s.a.w.) say: 'Whoever among you sees an evil, let him change it with his hand; if he cannot, then with his tongue; if he cannot, then with his heart—and that is the weakest of faith.'"
>
> (Sunan an-Nasaʾi 5008)

When we see something that is *munkar*, it should be recognised as an evil act—something that is not right. If we are the authority, change it. For example, if I am the one speaking in a lecture room, I have authority over it. If one of the audience was to speak out of turn or to insult another person, I would say, "Excuse me, please be quiet. If you don't want to be quiet, please leave." It is my authority, my place. If it is not my place, but I see someone doing something that is not right, I can go and whisper to someone responsible to take action. If we cannot change it ourselves, speak to the one who is responsible. We can also remind others with our tongues. If we cannot do either, the lowest level of *iman* is that in our hearts, we revolt and are repulsed by it. We hate it in our hearts. We say, "This is not right! I can't change it, I can't even speak about it. In my heart, I do not condone it, I do not normalise it, and I do not accept it."

This becomes an important test of what pure love and destructive love is.

As Muslims, we honour the legacy of our Prophet Muḥammad (s.a.w.) who calls us to a *fiṭrah*, who calls us to a healing, and who calls us to a natural state—natural biological intent, natural biological progression of increasing our community and *ummah*, and natural habit of marriage.

Marriage is a way of increasing love. We should not commit to each other without marriage. Sometimes, there will be a brother and a sister who practise the *deen* and they want to get married, but they connect to each other in an emotional sense more than they should. When it does not work or for whatever reason it does not fulfil, one of them is so devastated that it takes years for them to recover and the reason for it is self-inflicted. They had a love of what they wanted to do, wanted to feel, wanted to experience, wanted to save, wanted to hear, and wanted to have with each other in a way that is not permitted by Allah (s.w.t.). Then, when they feel broken as a consequence of committing to what they should not have done, they would ask, "Why do I find myself in this pain?"

I ask Allah (s.w.t.) to heal our hearts and to assist us in all of our affairs, *Allāhumma Āmīn*.

PART 3

Stories of Uplifting Love

CHAPTER 15

Love of the Truth

The Hidden Believer

Now, let us discuss the uplifting stories of love from the Qur'an. We do not want to end the book in gloom, do we?

One of the surahs in the Qur'an is called surah Ghafir. Another name for it is surah Mu'min, the hidden believer. Who was the hidden believer?

One of the family members of Firʿawn believed in Musa (a.s.) and everything he said, but he hid it. He did not want Firʿawn to know because it was going to bring his death, and his wife and children would become slaves. So, he tried to advise his people in secular ways. The hidden believer said, "Perhaps, listen to him. This man is only telling you to believe in God. He's not telling you he wants to take your gold and wealth. Maybe we should listen to what he has to say instead of making him an enemy straight away."

وَقَالَ رَجُلٌ مُّؤْمِنٌ مِّنْ ءَالِ فِرْعَوْنَ يَكْتُمُ
إِيمَٰنَهُۥٓ أَتَقْتُلُونَ رَجُلًا أَن يَقُولَ رَبِّىَ ٱللَّهُ
وَقَدْ جَآءَكُم بِٱلْبَيِّنَٰتِ مِن رَّبِّكُمْ ۖ وَإِن
يَكُ كَٰذِبًا فَعَلَيْهِ كَذِبُهُۥ ۖ وَإِن يَكُ صَادِقًا
يُصِبْكُم بَعْضُ ٱلَّذِى يَعِدُكُمْ ۖ إِنَّ ٱللَّهَ لَا
يَهْدِى مَنْ هُوَ مُسْرِفٌ كَذَّابٌ ﴿٢٨﴾

And a believing man from the family of Fir'awn who concealed his faith said, "Do you kill a man [merely] because he says, 'My Lord is Allah,' while he has brought you clear proofs from your Lord? And if he should be lying, then upon him is [the consequence of] his lie; but if he should be truthful, there will strike you some of what he promises you.

> Indeed, Allah does not guide one who is a transgressor and a liar."
>
> (Surah Ghafir, 40:28)

He said to the people, "If Musa is right, who would protect us from the punishment of Allah?" Then, Fir'awn said to his people, "I only advise you to do that which I think is good for myself, too."

يَٰقَوْمِ لَكُمُ ٱلْمُلْكُ ٱلْيَوْمَ ظَٰهِرِينَ فِى ٱلْأَرْضِ فَمَن يَنصُرُنَا مِنۢ بَأْسِ ٱللَّهِ إِن جَآءَنَا ۚ قَالَ فِرْعَوْنُ مَآ أُرِيكُمْ إِلَّا مَآ أَرَىٰ وَمَآ أَهْدِيكُمْ إِلَّا سَبِيلَ ٱلرَّشَادِ ﴿٢٩﴾

> "O' my people, sovereignty is yours today, [your being] dominant in the land. But who would protect us from the punishment of Allah if it came to us?" Fir'awn said, "I do not show you except what I see, and I do not guide you except to the way of right conduct."
>
> (Surah Ghafir, 40:29)

The Lesson

If we are not seated at the table where decisions are made, we are on the table and decisions are made about us. If we are not seated as part of the council and part of those who are able to give directions, then we are not going to be at the table—we are on the table.

We are going to be as the Prophet (s.a.w.) said, "There will come a time when people and nations gather against you the way they invite each other to a feast. They're going to feast on our *ummah*." The *ṣaḥabah* asked, "Because we're few in numbers? We can't defend ourselves?" The Prophet (s.a.w.) replied, "No. There will be many of you but you will be like the scum on the surface of a water body. The waves are moving you right and left. You have no determination, no power, and no word. You're not at the table, you're being eaten."

Narrated Thawban:

> The Prophet (s.a.w.) said: The people will soon summon one another to attack you as people when eating invite others to share their dish. Someone asked: Will that be because of our small numbers at that time? He replied:

> No, you will be numerous at that time, but you will be scum and rubbish like that carried down by a torrent, and Allah will take fear of you from the breasts of your enemy and last enervation into your hearts. Someone asked: What is *wahn* (enervation)? Messenger of Allah (s.a.w.): He replied: Love of the world and dislike of death.
>
> (Sunan Abi Dawud 4297)

Sometimes, there needs to be a believer who is righteous, who is not outward, and who is not, for example, the imam. I, as an imam, cannot be the representation in a political scene and I cannot be the one who has to make certain compromises, but there has to be someone who has a love for Allah (s.w.t.) and love for the Prophet (s.a.w.) who cannot be absent from every room. There has to be someone who stands up for Allah (s.w.t.), for the truth. It is a lesson of love for Allah (s.w.t.) even though it puts one in harm's way.

CHAPTER 16

Love of Patience

The Patience of the Wife of Firʿawn

Asiyah (r.a.) was the wife of Firʿawn, an evil man. She was granted a house in *Jannah* on account of her *ṣabr* in the face of tyranny.

Her *qadr* had put her in a place where it sapped all of her strength and all that she could say was, "O' Allah, build for me, on account of my patience here, an abode in *Jannah*."

وَضَرَبَ ٱللَّهُ مَثَلًا لِّلَّذِينَ ءَامَنُوا۟ ٱمْرَأَتَ
فِرْعَوْنَ إِذْ قَالَتْ رَبِّ ٱبْنِ لِى عِندَكَ بَيْتًا

فِى ٱلْجَنَّةِ وَنَجِّنِى مِن فِرْعَوْنَ وَعَمَلِهِۦ
وَنَجِّنِى مِنَ ٱلْقَوْمِ ٱلظَّـٰلِمِينَ ﴿١١﴾

And Allah presents an example of those who believed: the wife of Firʿawn, when she said, "My Lord, build for me near You a house in Paradise and save me from Firʿawn and his deeds and save me from the wrongdoing people."

(Surah at-Taḥrim, 66:11)

The Lesson

We are often tested with circumstances that are beyond our control, such as born into a circumstance, married into a circumstance, widowed into a circumstance and more. However, most of us have not come to a place in our lives where despair is overwhelming, *alḥamdulillāh*.

The conscience of a believer is to know that Allah's mercy, even in our difficulty, remains. One thing that we should remember is Allah (s.w.t.) always remains *ar-Raḥmān*, even when we are at our lowest point. Even so, we will never be at a lower point than the wife of Firʿawn, Asiyah (r.a.). It does not matter how bad your wife or husband is, you will never look at them and say, "*SubḥānAllāh*, Firʿawn." Never. But Asiyah (r.a.) got Firʿawn as her husband. She could only pray to Allah (s.w.t.) and remained *ṣabr*.

We need to look past the *dunya* for something greater in the *akhirah*. When we struggle in the *dunya*, it does not mean we should give up the struggle here, but we should know that our hope for justice is in the *akhirah*. The pursuit of justice in this *dunya* will never be achieved completely, even for Prophet Muḥammad (s.a.w.) whose justice will be made complete in the *akhirah*.

CHAPTER 17

Love for the *Ummah*

The Martyr

Our next uplifting story of love is from surah Yasin.

Three messengers, the *mursalun*, arrived in Antioch and they were telling people about believing in God:

إِذْ أَرْسَلْنَآ إِلَيْهِمُ ٱثْنَيْنِ فَكَذَّبُوهُمَا فَعَزَّزْنَا
بِثَالِثٍ فَقَالُوٓا۟ إِنَّآ إِلَيْكُم مُّرْسَلُونَ ﴿١٤﴾

When We sent to them two but they denied them, so We strengthened [them] with a third, and they said, "Indeed, we are messengers to you."

(Surah Yasin, 36:14)

Then, the people said, "No, we will kill you."

قَالُوٓاْ إِنَّا تَطَيَّرْنَا بِكُمْ ۖ لَئِن لَّمْ تَنتَهُواْ لَنَرْجُمَنَّكُمْ وَلَيَمَسَّنَّكُم مِّنَّا عَذَابٌ أَلِيمٌ ﴿١٨﴾

They said, "Indeed, we consider you a bad omen. If you do not desist, we will surely stone you, and there will surely touch you, from us, a painful punishment."

(Surah Yasin, 36:18)

After that, one of the people of the city, who was also from the people of the unbelievers, came from the other side of the city. He said, "Listen to the messengers."

وَجَآءَ مِنْ أَقْصَا ٱلْمَدِينَةِ رَجُلٌ يَسْعَىٰ قَالَ يَٰقَوْمِ ٱتَّبِعُواْ ٱلْمُرْسَلِينَ ﴿٢٠﴾ ٱتَّبِعُواْ مَن لَّا يَسْـَٔلُكُمْ أَجْرًا وَهُم مُّهْتَدُونَ ﴿٢١﴾ وَمَا لِىَ لَآ أَعْبُدُ ٱلَّذِى فَطَرَنِى وَإِلَيْهِ تُرْجَعُونَ

٢٢ ءَأَتَّخِذُ مِن دُونِهِۦٓ ءَالِهَةً إِن يُرِدْنِ
ٱلرَّحْمَٰنُ بِضُرٍّ لَّا تُغْنِ عَنِّى شَفَٰعَتُهُمْ شَيْـًٔا
وَلَا يُنقِذُونِ ٢٣ إِنِّىٓ إِذًا لَّفِى ضَلَٰلٍ مُّبِينٍ
٢٤ إِنِّىٓ ءَامَنتُ بِرَبِّكُمْ فَٱسْمَعُونِ ٢٥

And there came from the farthest end of the city a man, running. He said, "O' my people, follow the messengers. Follow those who do not ask of you [any] payment, and they are [rightly] guided. And why should I not worship He who created me and to whom you will be returned? Should I take other than Him [false] deities [while], if the Most Merciful intends for me some adversity, their intercession will not avail me at all, nor can they save me? Indeed, I would then be in manifest error. Indeed, I have believed in your Lord, so listen to me."

(Surah Yasin, 36:20-25)

Instead of listening, they killed him. As they killed him, Allah (s.w.t.) shared his thoughts. In the moment of his soul's departure, he said, "I wish my people could know how my Lord forgave me for a life of disservice to Him. I worshipped all these other things, but in a moment of my return to Allah, just a moment of recognising Allah, everything was forgiven. I wish these people, who now have earned even this great sin, could see and Allah has made me from those who are honoured and noble."

قِيلَ ٱدْخُلِ ٱلْجَنَّةَ ۖ قَالَ يَٰلَيْتَ قَوْمِى
يَعْلَمُونَ ﴿٢٦﴾ بِمَا غَفَرَ لِى رَبِّى وَجَعَلَنِى
مِنَ ٱلْمُكْرَمِينَ ﴿٢٧﴾

It was said, "Enter Paradise." He said, "I wish my people could know of how my Lord has forgiven me and placed me among the honoured."

(Surah Yasin, 36:26-27)

The Lesson

Sometimes, we need to speak up when it is difficult. Not all of us can be silent. I can speak up about one topic that I am familiar with, but I cannot speak about everything like other people can. There has to be someone who can.

Sometimes, the support that is granted to others in our *ummah* does not have to be vocal. It can be from behind the curtains, but can we be absent from issues that relate to our *ummah*? No. Should we be so impotent that I cannot even write an objection email, for example? That I cannot voice my opinion?

We often become so scared of the system that we become a part of it. May Allah (s.w.t.) protect us, *Allāhumma Āmīn*.

CHAPTER 18

Love of Forgiveness

The Forgiveness of Yusuf (a.s.)

Blood is thicker than water, but *iman* is more important than blood. Yusuf (a.s.) forgave his brothers, but not because they were his brothers. People often misunderstand this.

His brothers threw him in a well. They watched as a caravan came, then they sold him:

وَجَآءَتْ سَيَّارَةٌ فَأَرْسَلُوا۟ وَارِدَهُمْ فَأَدْلَىٰ
دَلْوَهُۥ ۖ قَالَ يَـٰبُشْرَىٰ هَـٰذَا غُلَـٰمٌ ۚ وَأَسَرُّوهُ
بِضَـٰعَةً ۚ وَٱللَّهُ عَلِيمٌۢ بِمَا يَعْمَلُونَ ١٩

وَشَرَوْهُ بِثَمَنٍۭ بَخْسٍ دَرَٰهِمَ مَعْدُودَةٍ
وَكَانُوا۟ فِيهِ مِنَ ٱلزَّٰهِدِينَ ﴿٢٠﴾

And there came a company of travellers; then they sent their water drawer, and he let down his bucket. He said, "Good news! Here is a boy." And they concealed him, [taking him] as merchandise; and Allah was Knowing of what they did. And they sold him for a reduced price—a few *dirhams*—and they were, concerning him, of those content with little.

(Surah Yusuf, 12:19-20)

They hid their evidence; they brought fake blood, put it on the cloth of Yusuf (a.s.) and they said to their father, "The wolf took him. All we could recover was his clothing."

وَجَآءُوٓ أَبَاهُمْ عِشَآءً يَبْكُونَ ﴿١٦﴾ قَالُوا۟
يَٰٓأَبَانَآ إِنَّا ذَهَبْنَا نَسْتَبِقُ وَتَرَكْنَا يُوسُفَ عِندَ
مَتَٰعِنَا فَأَكَلَهُ ٱلذِّئْبُ ۖ وَمَآ أَنتَ بِمُؤْمِنٍ

لَنَا وَلَوْ كُنَّا صَـٰدِقِينَ ﴿١٧﴾ وَجَآءُو عَلَىٰ
قَمِيصِهِۦ بِدَمٍ كَذِبٍ ۚ قَالَ بَلْ سَوَّلَتْ
لَكُمْ أَنفُسُكُمْ أَمْرًا ۖ فَصَبْرٌ جَمِيلٌ ۖ وَٱللَّهُ
ٱلْمُسْتَعَانُ عَلَىٰ مَا تَصِفُونَ ﴿١٨﴾

And they came to their father at night, weeping. They said, "O' our father, indeed we went racing each other and left Yusuf with our possessions, and a wolf ate him. But you would not believe us, even if we were truthful." And they brought upon his shirt false blood. [Yaʿqub] said, "Rather, your souls have enticed you to something, so patience is most fitting. And Allah is the one sought for help against that which you describe."

(Surah Yusuf, 12:16-18)

They let their father mourn with their lie until he became blind. That is how dark their hearts were:

وَتَوَلَّىٰ عَنْهُمْ وَقَالَ يَٰٓأَسَفَىٰ عَلَىٰ يُوسُفَ وَٱبْيَضَّتْ عَيْنَاهُ مِنَ ٱلْحُزْنِ فَهُوَ كَظِيمٌ ﴿٨٤﴾

And he turned away from them and said, "Oh, my sorrow over Yusuf," and his eyes became white from grief, for he was [of that] a suppressor.

(Surah Yusuf, 12:84)

And years later, Yusuf (a.s.) forgave them:

قَالَ لَا تَثْرِيبَ عَلَيْكُمُ ٱلْيَوْمَ ۖ يَغْفِرُ ٱللَّهُ لَكُمْ ۖ وَهُوَ أَرْحَمُ ٱلرَّٰحِمِينَ ﴿٩٢﴾

He said, "No blame will there be upon you today. May Allah forgive you; and He is the most merciful of the merciful."

(Surah Yusuf, 12:92)

The Lesson

He forgave them not because they were his brothers, not because blood is thicker than water, but because of *iman* in Allah's justice. *Iman* in something greater, past this *dunya*. There are certain things that Allah (s.w.t.) puts us through in life that even if we get justice, it would not be complete.

There was news about a Muslim brother from a few years ago. His son was a pizza delivery driver in America. He delivered pizzas to make a little bit of money. Unfortunately, he was robbed by gang members. They took his shoes, the pizza and twenty-six dollars from his pocket. They took his life for pizza, *subḥānAllāh*.

His father is an honourable Muslim man. While he was in the court with the murderer of his son, the judge said, "It's the sentencing time. The family of the deceased, of the murdered, we give you a chance to say what you feel in this moment about the loss of your son, about what happened." He said to the judge, "I want to hug this young man and I want him to know that I forgive him. Am I allowed?" The judge was taken aback. He said, "I want to hug him to let him know throughout the years he will spend in prison, that I have forgiven him for taking my son's life, but he can change himself and maybe he can find Allah."

Then, he hugged the person who murdered his son. He said, "Even if you were to spend a hundred years, it would not bring my boy back. And for that, I forgive you. The pain I will carry, but I forgive you in front of Allah." *SubḥānAllāh*, the power of being able to have that.

Forgiveness is not for them. It is for us, for our freedom. There are people in my life who I have forgiven and you should too. The freedom we get in being the one who is powerful enough to forgive:

'Abd Ṣamad reported:

> Al-Fuḍayl ibn 'Iyaḍ (r.a.h) said, "If a man comes to you complaining about another man, then say: O' brother, forgive him, as forgiveness is closer to righteousness. If he says my heart cannot tolerate forgiveness, but rather retaliation as Allah Almighty has commanded me, then say: If you must, do so in the best manner and retaliate with the same measure which you were afflicted, otherwise return to the door of forgiveness. Verily, the door of forgiveness is wider. Whoever forgives

> and sets things right, his reward is with Allah. The one who forgives will sleep comfortably in his bed and the one who avenges will toss and turn over his affairs."
>
> (Ḥilyat al-Awliya' 8/112)

It is liberating. When we forgive, we regain our power, our soul, our strength, our *iman*, our determination with Allah (s.w.t.), and we regain our life. We should know that our justice cannot be in this *dunya*.

Let me share with you another story: two or three days after the massacre in New Zealand, Dr. Omar Suleiman, myself and a few others flew down to assist the families of the victims. There was a Malaysian family who used to attend Dr. Omar's classes and they lost a son in the massacre. They asked Dr. Omar to lead the *janazah* prayer. I still remember the father, although I cannot remember his name. His back had bullet wounds because he shielded one of his sons from the shooting. He could only shield one of them; the other, he could not.

He was in a wheelchair. We carried his wheelchair closer to the *qabr* of his son because there was sand in the cemetery and he was in pain. He said, "I want to see his face one more time." As we were leaving with him after we said our *du'a'*, I remember he looked at me and said, "*Wallāhi*, I forgive the murderer." I said, "*SubḥānAllāh*, I can't forgive him." It was not my son, but I had seen the aftermath of the massacre so I said, "I can't forgive him." He hugged my hand, "*Wallāhi*, I forgive him." How Allah (s.w.t.) opened his heart, a man who has received injustice, to forgive such a person. May Allah (s.w.t.) give the family *khayr*, *Allāhumma Āmīn*. May Allah (s.w.t.) reunite us in *Jannah* and reunite them with their loved ones in *Jannah*, *Allāhumma Āmīn*.

The power of Yusuf (a.s.) is what was remembered when Prophet Muḥammad (s.a.w.) entered Makkah after the conquest. The people of Quraysh were scared of him, then he forgave them:

Al-Qasim ibn Salam reported:

> When his enemies came to the Ka'bah, they were holding onto its door and the Prophet (s.a.w.) said, "What do you say? What do you think?" They said three times, "We say you are the son of our brother." The Prophet said, "I say to you as Yusuf said to his brothers: No blame upon you today. Allah will forgive you,

> for He is the most merciful of the merciful." (Surah Yusuf, 12:92) In another narration, the Prophet said to them, "Go, you are free."
>
> (al-Sunan al-Kubra 18275)

May Allah (s.w.t.) grant us the sunnah of Yusuf (a.s.) and allow us to forgive in our hearts, but remember not to be rehurt. There is a difference between forgiving and allowing injustice to occur again in front of us. This is not the sunnah of the Prophet (s.a.w.). We forgive and then seek justice with Allah (s.w.t.).

For example, I can forgive you and then take you to court to pay me back what you owe. *Wallāhi*, in front of Allah (s.w.t.), I forgive you. But as long as you are breathing and able, and you owe me my right, I will pursue it.

There is a difference between forgiving others in front of Allah (s.w.t.) and letting them hurt us again, or letting them get away with it and do it to others. We can pursue them but we can also ask for our justice in a higher court with Allah (s.w.t.).

Q&A

QUESTION 1

Nabi Musa (a.s.), utterly disappointed, he made *du'a'* for Allah (s.w.t.) to separate himself and Nabi Harun (a.s.) from his transgressing people. Did he give up on his mission and when do we stop reminding the recalcitrant and uninspired especially amongst family?

Answer: First, let us look at what Allah (s.w.t.) advised our Prophet Muḥammad (s.a.w.) about Yunus (a.s.). The first story in the Qur'an shared with our Prophet (s.a.w.) is the story of Yunus (a.s.). One of the first things that Allah (s.w.t.) said to the Prophet (s.a.w.) was, "O' Muḥammad, look at the example of Nabi Yunus who when I told him to stay with his people, when he saw the signs of My punishment coming, he left. Don't do this yourself."

فَٱصْبِرْ لِحُكْمِ رَبِّكَ وَلَا تَكُن كَصَاحِبِ
ٱلْحُوتِ إِذْ نَادَىٰ وَهُوَ مَكْظُومٌ ﴿٤٨﴾

Then be patient for the decision of your Lord, [O' Muḥammad], and be not like the companion of the fish [i.e., Yunus] when he called out while he was distressed.

(Surah al-Qalam, 68:48)

Now, the *du'a'* of Musa (a.s.) that we are referring to here is:

قَالَ رَبِّ إِنِّى لَآ أَمْلِكُ إِلَّا نَفْسِى وَأَخِى ۖ فَٱفْرُقْ بَيْنَنَا وَبَيْنَ ٱلْقَوْمِ ٱلْفَٰسِقِينَ ﴿٢٥﴾

[Musa] said, "My Lord, indeed I do not possess [i.e., control] except myself and my brother, so part us from the defiantly disobedient people."

(Surah al-Ma'idah, 5:25)

Musa (a.s.) in making this *du'a'* asking Allah (s.w.t.) to save him, Harun (a.s.) and his few believers was not because he was giving up and asking Allah (s.w.t.) to admit the disobedient into Hell. He did not say, "O' Allah, allow us to enter *Jannah*, allow us to die with *iman* and let this wretched people go to Hell." But it was because of his fear of the descent of Allah's punishment at that time, as the disobedient did not obey Allah's command for *jihad*. So one of the reasons why Allah (s.w.t.) caused Musa (a.s.) and his people to wander the desert for forty years was that it naturally killed off all of those who worshipped the golden calf:

قَالَ فَإِنَّهَا مُحَرَّمَةٌ عَلَيْهِمْ ۛ أَرْبَعِينَ سَنَةً ۛ يَتِيهُونَ فِى ٱلْأَرْضِ ۚ فَلَا تَأْسَ عَلَى ٱلْقَوْمِ ٱلْفَٰسِقِينَ ﴿٢٦﴾

[Allah] said, "Then indeed, it is forbidden to them for forty years [in which] they will wander throughout the land. So do not grieve over the defiantly disobedient people."

(Surah al-Ma'idah, 5:26)

Those who crossed from Egypt, forty years later became worthy—a new generation was born from them, travelling throughout the earth with Musa (a.s.), throughout the deserts of Arabia and Sinai until they were worthy of crossing into the blessed land, *al-Arḍ al-Muqaddasah*.

Next, Allah (s.w.t.) gives us the example of Nuḥ (a.s.). Imagine if you are a Prophet of Allah (s.w.t.)

and you are telling people that Islam is right and the truth. Then your son, your own flesh and blood, is sitting in front of you and says, "Don't listen to this old man. Don't listen to anything he says." Or if I stand on a *minbar* as an imam and I am telling people, "Everyone, this is what is right." Then I look outside the window where my son is walking by and he is doing everything opposite to what I tell others. This is the kind of pressure that Nuḥ (a.s.) was facing and it is very difficult.

Nuḥ (a.s.) was building a ship in the desert and people were ridiculing him:

وَٱصْنَعِ ٱلْفُلْكَ بِأَعْيُنِنَا وَوَحْيِنَا وَلَا تُخَٰطِبْنِى فِى ٱلَّذِينَ ظَلَمُوٓا۟ ۚ إِنَّهُم مُّغْرَقُونَ ﴿٣٧﴾ وَيَصْنَعُ ٱلْفُلْكَ وَكُلَّمَا مَرَّ عَلَيْهِ مَلَأٌ مِّن قَوْمِهِۦ سَخِرُوا۟ مِنْهُ ۚ قَالَ إِن تَسْخَرُوا۟ مِنَّا فَإِنَّا نَسْخَرُ مِنكُمْ كَمَا تَسْخَرُونَ ﴿٣٨﴾

"And construct the ship under Our observation and Our inspiration and do not address Me concerning those who have wronged; indeed,

> they are [to be] drowned." And he constructed the ship, and whenever an assembly of the eminent of his people passed by him, they ridiculed him. He said, "If you ridicule us, then we will ridicule you just as you ridicule."
>
> (Surah Hud, 11:37-38)

There was no rain, no river and no water, so it made no sense to them and they thought he was crazy. But Allah (s.w.t.) ordered him and he listened. Then, the earth was commanded by Allah (s.w.t.) to erupt with water. The heavens rained down torrential rains. Everyone was trying to get on the ship, but Nuḥ (a.s.) had the order to prevent them except the believers:

حَتَّىٰٓ إِذَا جَآءَ أَمْرُنَا وَفَارَ ٱلتَّنُّورُ قُلْنَا ٱحْمِلْ فِيهَا مِن كُلٍّ زَوْجَيْنِ ٱثْنَيْنِ وَأَهْلَكَ إِلَّا مَن سَبَقَ عَلَيْهِ ٱلْقَوْلُ وَمَنْ ءَامَنَ ۚ وَمَآ ءَامَنَ مَعَهُۥٓ إِلَّا قَلِيلٌ ﴿٤٠﴾

> [So it was], until when Our command came and the oven overflowed, We said, "Load upon it [i.e., the ship] of each [creature] two

> mates and your family, except those about whom the word [i.e., decree] has preceded, and [include] whoever has believed." But none had believed with him, except a few.
>
> (Surah Hud, 11:40)

The *du'a'* of Nuḥ (a.s.) is where he said, "O'Allah, give me the permission to not allow them on the ship. Their sins are what is going to destroy them."

وَقَالَ نُوحٌ رَّبِّ لَا تَذَرْ عَلَى ٱلْأَرْضِ مِنَ ٱلْكَٰفِرِينَ دَيَّارًا ﴿٢٦﴾

> And Nuḥ said, "My Lord, do not leave upon the earth from among the disbelievers an inhabitant."
>
> (Surah Nuḥ, 71:26)

So when his son was there, he said, "My son, come on the ship but don't be a disbeliever. I can't let you come on the ship unless you believe in Allah."

وَهِىَ تَجْرِى بِهِمْ فِى مَوْجٍ كَٱلْجِبَالِ وَنَادَىٰ نُوحٌ ٱبْنَهُۥ وَكَانَ فِى مَعْزِلٍ يَـٰبُنَىَّ ٱرْكَب مَّعَنَا وَلَا تَكُن مَّعَ ٱلْكَـٰفِرِينَ ﴿٤٢﴾

And it sailed with them through waves like mountains, and Nuḥ called to his son who was apart [from them], "O' my son, come aboard with us and be not with the disbelievers."

(Surah Hud, 11:42)

The first principle that I establish for this question is that people will live their own lives but we do not change the religion to accommodate them. A person might live their own life in a sinful way, make their own choices or make their own path, but we do not make the illegitimate legitimate. We do not change the haram to halal. We do not pervert what we know to be the truth as false or the false as truth just because we love them. Just because it is our son, daughter, wife, husband, mother or father, it does not mean we are allowed to change the religion. However, we can open the door, we can have our hands out and invite them in, but it is conditional.

The second principle is we never close a door that cannot be opened again. Only Allah (s.w.t.) closes that door. What is that door? Death. As long as a person has in their life the ability—even on their deathbed—to say, "I come back to Allah," even with their eyes, do not close the door. We should give them that opportunity. We should open the door, put our hands out and invite them. We are not going to accept the haram but we should not exclude them, especially if they are willing to come back to the truth. This is where only Allah (s.w.t.) judges.

QUESTION 2

When do we let go and let Allah (s.w.t.) alone that opens someone's heart to Islam?

Answer: I leave with you this hadith of the Prophet (s.a.w.). This hadith has been life-changing for me in my approach to *da'wah*:

> Abu Hurayrah reported God's Messenger as saying, "There were two men among the *Bani Isra'il* who loved one another, one of whom engaged ardently in worship while the other called himself a sinner. The former began to say, 'Refrain from what you are doing,' and the other would reply, 'Let me alone with my Lord.' One day he found him committing a sin which he considered serious and said, 'Refrain'; to which he replied, 'Let me alone with my Lord. Were you sent to watch over me?' He then said, 'I swear by God that God will never pardon you, nor will He bring you into Paradise.' God then sent to them an angel who took their spirits, and they came together into His presence. To the sinner He said, 'Enter Paradise by My mercy'; and to

> the other He said, 'Can you forbid My mercy to My servant?' He replied, 'No, my Lord.' Then He said, 'Take him away to Hell.'"
>
> (Mishkat al-Maṣabiḥ 2347)

The Prophet (s.a.w.) said that in the time before our time, in the nation before our nation, there were two people who became closer than brothers. They became like brothers in front of Allah (s.w.t.) for their relationship with Allah (s.w.t.). One of them was *ṣaliḥ*, a righteous man who did everything outwardly right. On the other hand, his best friend was *muqṣir*. He was always a few steps behind from where he should be and where he should attain to.

The first one, the *ṣaliḥ*, said to the *muqṣir*, "Stop this lifestyle of yours. You will never be forgiven by Allah. You have no hope of Paradise if you continue acting this way." His friend who loved Allah (s.w.t.) but was sinful replied, "Leave me to Allah. He didn't make you my policeman in life, He didn't set you to be my judge, jury and executioner. Leave me to a moment with Allah. Perhaps just give me some hope."

When they died, they were brought together in

front of Allah (s.w.t.) and questioned by Allah (s.w.t.) in front of each other. Allah (s.w.t.) said to the first one, "Did you say to him I will never forgive him? Did you say to him he has no hope in *Jannah*? Did I give My power of decision to you? Did I give knowledge to you who is in *Jannah* and who isn't? What gave you this power of authority to say he's going to Hell? Who made you the judge? Witness today, I forgive him whilst you are going to be held back and cleansed for putting despair into his heart."

Never be the door that closes to another person's *hidayah*. Never be the frown that turns a person away from walking into a lecture. Never be the one who looks at someone whose *ḥijab* is not perfect that you make them feel uncomfortable. Never be the one who makes someone—who is searching with an honest question or a silly question—feel stupid for having asked it, that they never ask again and never seek Allah (s.w.t.) anymore, because on the Day of Judgement, we will stand in front of Allah (s.w.t.) and we will be questioned, "Why did you become the barrier between this man's heart and My *Jannah*? Why did you prevent their entitlement to repentance?"

The Conclusion

There is a hadith about a man who killed ninety-nine people and he asked a worshipping person, "I've killed many people in my life. Will God forgive me?" The reply that he got was, "No, you're a murderer. Why would God forgive you?" So he killed him and made it a hundred:

> Narrated Abu Sa'id al-Khudri:
>
> The Prophet (s.a.w.) said, "Amongst the men of *Bani Isra'il* there was a man who had murdered ninety-nine persons. Then he set out asking (whether his repentance could be accepted or not). He came upon a monk and asked him if his repentance could be accepted. The monk replied in the negative and so the man killed him. He kept on asking until a man advised to go to such-and-such village. (So he left for it) but death overtook him on the way. While dying, he turned his chest towards that village (where he had hoped his repentance would be accepted), and so the angels of mercy and the angels of punishment quarrelled amongst themselves regarding him. Allah ordered the village (towards which he was going) to come

> closer to him, and ordered the village (whence he had come), to go far away, and then He ordered the angels to measure the distances between his body and the two villages. So he was found to be one span closer to the village (he was going to). So he was forgiven."
>
> (Ṣaḥiḥ al-Bukhari 3470)

He made it a hundred because in his mind, he thought, "What do I have to lose?" If people in our lives feel that they have no hope of redemption and they feel that as a sinner, they cannot make it to *Jannah*, they would think they have nothing to lose. Why should they even try? Who should they try for? If they have no hope and no one will ever forgive them, if no one will ever overlook their sin, if no one will ever forget it, if no one will ever allow them an opportunity to redeem themselves, then they would think, "To Hell with the rest of the world as well!" So do not be the reason a person turns back from where they were going towards Allah (s.w.t.).

Arabic Glossary

'Adl	- Just
Akhirah	- The afterlife
al-Arḍ al-Muqaddasah	- Holy Land
al-Kawthar	- Name of a river in Paradise
al-mahfuẓ fiṣ-ṣudur wal-maṣaḥif	- Guarded and protected in the heart of the Muslim community and in the *muṣḥaf*
al-munazzal 'ala Muḥammad	- Revelation brought down to Muḥammad (s.a.w.)
al-muta'abbadu bitilawatih	- Rewarded for each recitation
Alḥamdulillāh	- Praise be to Allah
Allāhu Akbar	- Allah is the Greatest
Allāhumma Āmīn	- O' Allah, accept our prayer
'Amal	- Deeds

ar-Raḥmān	- The Most Merciful (one of Allah's 99 names)
ar-Razzāq	- The Provider (one of Allah's 99 names)
Ash-hadu allā 'ilāha 'illa-llāh wā ashhadu 'anna muḥammadur-rasūlullāh	- I bear witness that there is no god besides Allah and I bear witness that Muḥammad is the Messenger of Allah
'Aṣr	- Afternoon prayer, one of the five mandatory Islamic prayers
Athar	- Track/footprint
Ayah	- Qur'an verse
Bani Isra'il	- The children or descendants of the Isra'il tribe
Barakah	- Blessings
Bashar	- Human being
Bid'ah	- Innovation in Islamic practices and matters
Da'wah	- A call to embrace Islam
Deen	- Religion

Dhikr	- Remembrance of Allah
Du'a'	- Supplication
Dunya	- The temporal world and its earthly concerns and possessions
Fiṭrah	- The innate human nature
Ḥajj	- Pilgrimage
Ḥarf	- Letter/alphabet
Ḥasad	- Envy
Ḥasanah	- A good deed
Ḥasanat	- Plural of *ḥasanah*
Hidayah	- Guidance
Ḥijab	- A covering for the hair and neck
Iblis	- The chief of the wicked devil
Ilah	- God
Iman	- Faith
Insan	- Human
Inshā'Allāh	- If Allah wills
Iqamah	- Call to stand for prayer
'Isha'	- Night prayer, one of the five mandatory Islamic prayers

Jalal	- The majesty
Janazah	- Funeral
Jannah	- Paradise/Heaven
Jihad	- War/a meritorious struggle or effort/to struggle or strive against injustice, barriers and odds
Jinn	- Unseen creatures created before Adam (a.s.)
Kalamullāh	- The Book of Allah
Kalimullāh	- One who conversed with Allah
Khalifah	- Successor/deputy/vicegerent
Khalil	- Close friend/ companion
Khayr	- Good
Khuld	- Eternity
Kufr	- Ingratitude/disbelief
Kursi	- Throne
Lā ʾilāha ʾilla-llāh muḥammadur-rasūlu-llāh	- There is no god besides Allah and Muḥammad is the Messenger of Allah
Maghrib	- Sunset prayer, one of the five mandatory Islamic prayers

Maḫfuẓ	- Preserved
Malik	- Sovereign
Man jadda wajada	- Whoever strives shall succeed
Minbar	- Pulpit
Mu'adhdhin	- The person who gives the call to prayer at a mosque
Munkar	- Immoral behaviour
Muqṣir	- The person who can still improve and change
Mursalun	- Messengers
Muṣḥaf	- A written copy of the Qur'an
Nadim	- Regretful
Nasa	- To forget
Niʿmah	- Blessing
Nisyan	- Forgetfulness
Nur	- Light
Qabr	- Grave
Qadr	- Fate
Rabb	- Lord

Raḥmah - Compassion/mercy

Ṣabr - Patience

Ṣadaqah - Charity

Ṣaḥabah - Companions of the Prophet (s.a.w.)

Ṣalah - Prayer

Ṣaliḥ - Pious

Shaddah - Strength; one of the diacritical marks in Arabic alphabet that doubles the consonant it is written on

Shari'ah - Allah's immutable divine law

Shirk - Idolatry/polytheism

Shurṭah - Police

SubḥānAllāh - Glory be to Allah

Sujud - Prostration

s.w.t. - The Mighty and The Majestic

Tafsir - Interpretation

Tahlil - A form of *dhikr*

Tajwid - The set of rules determining how the words of the Qur'an are pronounced

Tanzil - Revelation

Tasbiḥ	- A form of *dhikr*
Tawakkul	- Reliance on Allah
Tawbah	- Repentance
Tawrah	- The revelation received by Musa (a.s.)
Tazkiyah	- Purification of the self
'Ujub	- Self-love/vanity/self-conceit
'Ulama'	- The body of religious scholars who are versed theoretically and practically in the Muslim sciences
Ummah	- Muslim community
'Umrah	- Minor pilgrimage
Ustadh	- Teacher
Waḥyu	- Revelation
Wallāhi	- I swear to Allah
Wallāhu a'lam	- Allah knows best
Zakah	- Almsgiving
Zina	- Unlawful sexual intercourse

www.ingramcontent.com/pod-product-compliance
Lightning Source LLC
LaVergne TN
LVHW061614070526
838199LV00078B/7279
9789672844440